NICE THINGS PEOPLE SAID
ABOUT *GRADES, GIRLS AND GOD*

"All of us are on a journey. With every image today clamoring for their attention, the journey for teenage men might have it the hardest. In *Grades, Girls, and God* - Andy provides a thoughtful, God-inspired path that enables young men to become the man God created them to be. This is a needed book! It's a timely blueprint that will inspire the next generation of fathers and husbands."

Tomas M. Kane
Author of *Protect Yourself at College, Priests are People, Too!*

"High school is a deeply formational time. The choices we make in those early years set us on a path for the rest of our lives. Andy's heart to help young men comes through loud and clear on every page. His book serves as a guide to help teens to make wise choices and successfully navigate trials and temptations."

Kary Oberbrunner,
Author of *Elixir Project, Your Secret Name,*
Day Job to Dream Job, The Deeper Path

GRADES, GIRLS, AND GOD

GRADES, GIRLS, AND GOD

HOW TO SURVIVE AND THRIVE
IN HIGH SCHOOL AS A CHRISTIAN MAN

ANDY BUCKWALTER

ꓵAUTHOR
ACADEMY elite

Printed in the United States of America

Published by Author Academy Elite
P.O. Box 43, Powell, OH 43035
www.AuthorAcademyElite.com

Paperback: 978-1-946114-42-6
Hardback: 978-1-946114-43-3
Library of Congress Control Number: 2017902197

Author Academy Elite, Powell, Ohio

To my beautiful wife Leann,
Thank you for your support and encouragement
I love you eternity

HERE'S WHAT'S IN THIS BOOK:

DON'T SKIP THE INTRO!

So I Get It

Your youth pastor or mom or someone gave you this book. You probably didn't go to Amazon yourself and buy it. (If you did, thanks!) But the odds are pretty good that someone gave you this book, and now you're thinking, "Why on earth would they give me this book?" You probably don't like to read, and even if you do like to read, it's a well-guarded secret between you and your librarian.

Don't worry, I won't tell anyone I saw you reading.

But you should rest assured knowing that I wrote this book just for you. You're probably in high school, or maybe you will be in a few years, or maybe you were a year or two ago. But for the rest of the time, I'm going to just assume high school age.

Here's what I know about you. Every day you get up, and you go to school. You don't really like school, but if you're honest; it's not so terrible. At least you get summers off. You go to church sometimes, probably a few times a month. Maybe you're involved in your youth group or a small group Bible study of some kind. You probably know a lot of church answers. If not, don't worry about it, this book is for you too. Here's why I wrote it.

The Church (capital C) is doing a pretty poor job with you right now. We don't really understand you. Somewhere between gross youth group games involving filling your mouth with marshmallows, and all night Halo competitions, we've forgotten to talk about real issues that you're really going to face in high school. We're not really preparing you to be the man God has called you to be. That's why I wrote this book. I sat down and thought about as many areas as I could that I wish I had been prepared for better in high school. And now, I want to share with you what I wish I had known!

So Now What?

Now we get started. This book is going to be your tool to not only survive high school, but to thrive there. We're going to discuss a bunch of hard hitting topics in this book. These to be specific:

What it means to be a man of God
How to wrestle with what you believe
Having a Focus time (whatever that is)
Dating
Pornography
Sex
Bullying
Knowing your value
Forgiveness

Starting to sound real enough for you? Of course, there are more things we could talk about. And I hope we do someday.

But for now, this book should get us started. Before we do, here are a few things to know about this book.

This book is intentionally short. I know you're busy. What with the video games, and sports, and clubs, and fantasy football, and all of the other important things you have going on. And I know you're not supposed to like reading. So I made the chapters short and concise to get right to the point. That being said, take the time to read it. The chapters are like 7-10 pages long. If you read one and a half pages every day, you can finish a chapter a week. That's only like three minutes a day. So read the whole thing. I didn't include anything I don't think is important.

At the end of each chapter you're going to see something called action steps. These are questions and missions to help you get the most out of each chapter. Take the time to fill them out and do them. Again, I know you're like super busy, but I really think going through them will help you out. They're not long, and they will make a difference.

I'm really glad that you're reading this book. Just know that every word of this book has been showered with prayer. And my prayer for you is that you'll open this book and really challenge yourself to grow. Really challenge yourself to make your faith your own. And be open to becoming the man God created you to be.

You ready?

Let's get started.

WELCOME TO NO MAN'S LAND

This Book Starts Off By Talking About Guns And Stuff

In WWI weaponry took a real turn for the better. Or worse depending on how you look at it. Either way, new technology was created that made it way easier for soldiers to kill each other. So, something interesting would happen. Soldiers would engage one another, but quickly realize that the number of bullets flying around them, was far higher than they were comfortable with.

So they would duck and cover behind anything they could. A bush, a rock, a tree, even just a slightly raised part of the ground, and they would start digging. They would take out a shovel and just start piling dirt up in front of them to hide behind. And as the dirt in front of them got larger, so did the hole beneath them. And pretty soon, they had dug their first trench.

This is pretty much how trench warfare got started. The technology was just too powerful to openly fight each other with, so both sides of the war would dig these trenches to protect themselves with. While trenches were not glamourous, they meant safety and survival to those soldiers huddled down in them. From your trench, you could duck and hide to take shelter, or you could protect your body while you shot at the enemy from the trench.

So both sides built these trenches. Do you see the problem here? Both sides are hiding in the trenches safely. How does anyone win one of these fights? Don't they just become an eternal standoff of trying to shoot the other guys down in their trench? Not exactly. Periodically, one side would send a group of soldiers running across the field in between the trenches to try to get close enough to the enemy to open fire.

Generally, they would do this by shooting large artillery fire towards the enemy to get them to duck down and cover. This would give the soldiers a window to run across the field between the trenches and attack their enemies. Sounds great in theory, but this almost never worked. What inevitably happened was that these men would take off running, only to get mowed down by the enemy before they could even get close.

So, this stretch of land between the trenches was a terrible place to find oneself. Not only was it treacherous from taking bullets and artillery fire over the course of months, but it was booby trapped. Land mines, grenades, and barbed wire were aimlessly thrown into this terrain to keep enemy soldiers at bay. The weapons, helmets, and bodies of fallen soldiers littered the ground adding the distinct stench of death to the already pungent aroma of mud, sweat, blood, and fear. It was a place of death feared by all. And because of the terrible conditions inhabiting this stretch of land-in between trenches, it earned a nickname.

No Man's Land

No man's land. The terrible stretch of land that had to be traveled if victory was to be won. The darkness guarded on either side by safety.

Imagine taking that first step. Climbing out on top of the trench. That beautiful trench that you dug to keep you safe. It might have been your home for the last week. Or month. Or maybe just hours. But it was safe. And now you stand, in front of that same enemy that sent you diving for cover. And you stare directly ahead at him. And begin your charge. Into no man's land. Into the unknown. Out of safety.

Out Of The Trench

"I didn't know this was a history book..." It's not, there's a point. I told you this story because I think no man's land is a great description for where you find yourself today. I think there are a lot of parallels between no man's land and high school. Hear me out.

You were a kid. You were in elementary school with all of your friends, and things were good. The bus came to get you in the morning, and there was a sticker with your name on it telling you where to sit. Your teacher was kind and helpful, you had like twelve snacks a day, one nap, and virtually unlimited recess time. Your friends were all nice most of the time, you played tag and hide and seek. You would go home and watch cartoons, or go outside to play, or play video games, and maybe have another snack. You eat dinner, take a bath, and call it a night. Nothing could ever go wrong; everything was great. You were content. You were safe. You were in your trench.

Then something terrible happened. *Middle School.* Suddenly, nothing in the whole world made sense. You were angry all the time, and you had no idea why. You were also sad, and worried, and stressed, and self-conscious a lot of the time, but you only showed that you were angry. The bus started coming way too early, you had eight teachers every day, and they were all out to get you. Your friends got moodier than you were, and the only game you played anymore was gossip about the girls. You were hungry all the time, but there were no snacks to be had. You would go home and it would be time for soccer practice, or chess club, or jazz band, or swim team or something. Then when you finally got home, you still had homework, and your annoying parents wouldn't let you watch television until it was done. Out of the trench.

And now you find yourself in high school. And all of that is still true. Plus you have feelings for girls that just don't make sense to anyone; you're still growing which hurts, and makes you really hungry, which makes you really grouchy. You're somehow exhausted and wired all of the time. You have an ocean of testosterone flowing through your veins. You have to get good grades. You're obsessed with girls. And somewhere in all of that, you're supposed to fit God into your life.

No Man's Land

Maybe you were raised in church, maybe you're new to this whole God thing; it doesn't matter. I'm really glad you're reading this book. For one thing, I'm glad you're reading *anything* and not just watching Youtube videos. But I'm glad you're reading this because I really think a book like this can help make a difference for you in high school. I want to help you do more than just survive high school. I want you to thrive. I want you to become the man God created you to be.

I call high school no man's land for three main reasons.

1) It's located in between two areas of safety.
2) It's a dangerous place to be; and
3) The truth is, a lot of people that enter it, die there.

Between Safety

High school is located between the safety of being a child and the safety of being an adult. But right now, you're stuck in this weird middle ground. People are telling you to act like an adult, but are treating you like a kid. They're telling you to be in the moment and prepare for your future. They want you to enjoy being young, but they keep making you read Shakespeare. It's a weird time. You're kind of stuck in-between two major stages of life. Or at least, it can feel that way. We're going to talk a lot later about how this is a really important time of your life, where you can really make a difference for yourself and others. But it's a weird time of your life, and I recognize that.

Danger

No man's land was a dangerous place. And so is high school. I don't mean physically of course. Hopefully your school is a safe place that you can go to without worry. But what I mean by dangerous is the temptations that come with being in high school. You know the ones I'm talking about. There are girls and there's cheating, and there's drinking, and there's pornography, and sex, and drugs, and there's fighting, and so many angry people, and there's gossiping, and rumors flying here and there… You get the point. It can be rough out there. And that's part of the reason for the third aspect of no man's land.

Game Over

A lot of people that enter no man's land die. Again, not a literal death. But I've seen it many times. A lot of guys enter high school with a pretty solid faith in God. Maybe they attend church, maybe they volunteer, and perhaps they go to their youth group. But somewhere between the trenches, they lose it. Whether it's sports, or girls, or partying, or falling in with friends that pull them away. A lot of guys slowly slide into apathy when it comes to God along the way. And unfortunately, a lot of young men completely abandon their relationship with God and their faith altogether in high school, middle school, or early college.

High school, much like no man's land, can be a treacherous place. There are temptations, struggles and challenges that just don't occur before or after that make it so unique. But it doesn't have to be a battlefield. No man's land doesn't have to be the end. High school can be a great time for you to grow. It can be a great time for you to begin changing the world. It can be where you decide to become the man God created you to be. And I'm excited for you.

Your Situation is...Well, Complicated

High school can be a frustrating place to be. Right now, virtually everything you're doing is prep work. You're just preparing for the future. Which is an important time, and a great time, but can also be a frustrating time. Because you're a man, there's probably this inborn sense in you that tells you that you need to be doing something. You feel like you're ready now. You feel like you're ready to take on the world. You want to be kicking down the door, rescuing the girl, and saving the world. You don't want to prepare. You want to do. And there are some things you're ready to do, but for some things, you need to keep working.

Think about it. You're in school to learn. You're taking guitar lessons to get better. You go to sports practice to hone your skills. You're practicing how to drive. You're preparing for college. You're figuring out what you want to do with your life. You're learning a new language in case you accidentally move to another country. You have a job to learn responsibility and gain an appreciation for the dollar. Pretty much everything you're doing at this stage of your life is preparation for when you're older. And again, that can feel frustrating, but it's a good thing.

But something we, as the Church (capital C), have done a poor job of preparing you for is being a man of God. We're not really doing a very good job of preparing you to be the man God wants you to be. We've kind of let you down. You're preparing for everything in your life, your career, your relationships, your decision making, but we don't teach you what it means to be a man of God, or how to become one.

But there is an important distinction that we need to make here. And this is critical, so I'm going to put it in bold typeface.

You are already a man of God.

You already are. Did you catch that? Much like you are already a man; you are already a man of God. And just like you have some prep work to do in high school, you have some prep work to do in your walk with God. But do not think for one minute that you will someday be a man of God. If you only take one thing from this book, let it be that.

So much of your life right now is preparation. People keep telling you that you are going to be ready. After you finish high school, after you make varsity, after you've been driving for six months, after you're eighteen…

You are a man of God. Right now.

It's not that you will be. It's not that someday you'll be ready. Right now, God has big things in store for you. Right now, God has a plan for you. Right now, you are a man in God's eyes. The key is to become more and more like the man God wants you to be. And less and less like the one society has taught you to emulate.

Let's Do This

So that's your situation. You are a high school aged man, who is trapped in a system that tells you to prepare for everything, except how to be a man of God. The rest of this book is going to help you prep. It's going to start diving into real issues to help you really grow and challenge yourself. But I have one challenge for you before we move on.

Tell someone you're reading this.

Tell someone. Maybe a friend of yours, maybe somebody at youth group, maybe your dad or youth pastor. But tell someone. This will help you for several reasons. For one, it will keep you accountable to keep reading. But more importantly, it will give you someone to bounce ideas off of. It will let you wrestle with the content even further. If you're already reading this as part of a group, that's great! Still tell someone. Invite them to your group. If you're reading solo, tell someone that you're doing it.

Check out the action steps, and let's move on.

Action Steps

What are some "land-mines" that you find in high school? (peer pressure, drugs, sex...)

_____

_____

_____

_____

What are some things you are preparing for? What are some things you already feel ready to do?

_____

_____

_____

_____

What are your goals for this book?

_____

_____

_____

_____

Who are you going to tell about this book? Text them right now.

_____

_____

_____

_____

BE A MAN, "WAIT, WHAT DOES THAT MEAN?"

Jesus Vs Chuck Norris

So I used to work in youth ministry in a variety of ways. I was a youth pastor for several years, but one summer, I got the opportunity to work at a Christian summer camp (FUGE camps for those of you interested). One of my roles in this camp was to lead a track every afternoon called, "For guys only." And it was exactly that. It was a small group of teenage guys that got together for an hour in the afternoon just to talk about life. We talked about a lot of things, most of which revolved around girls, but covered a wide variety of things they were experiencing and would experience in life.

One of the first things I asked them to do was make a list of the manliest men on the planet; past and present. We had a lot of fun doing this, but I did have two rules. You couldn't include Jesus, and you couldn't include Chuck Norris, because those are just trump cards. But they put together great lists including guys like John Cena, Abraham Lincoln, Sean Connery, Jason Statham, Theodore Roosevelt, Arnold Schwarzenegger, The Rock... the list went on.

Then I asked them why they picked these men. Most of them hadn't really thought about this. They just picked guys they thought were awesome. So I asked them to define what it means to be manly by society's standards. Here are some of the traits they came up with:

A manly man is strong and tall
A manly man can hunt
A manly man doesn't show emotion
He can get a lot of girls
He has a lot of money
He can beat people up
He saves the day
He can drink a lot
He wears nice clothes
He has a beard
He has a cool car and can fix that car
He is athletic...

This is what it means to be a man in society's eyes. Now, don't get me wrong, there's nothing wrong with being some of these things. (I wouldn't start trying to grow a beard just yet). But the lists we made every week didn't really reflect what it meant to be a man in God's eyes.

Redefining Manliness

So something we need to establish right from the beginning is this: *God's definition of what it means to be a man is very different from society's definition of what it means to be a man.* Did you catch that? God's version of manliness looks very different from society's version. And if that's the case, then we need to get a new definition of what it means to be a man.

God doesn't care if you're tall. He doesn't care how much you bench. He doesn't care if you're on the football team. He doesn't care if you have a beard. None of the things the world tells us makes a man, are important to God. So one of the first things that we need to do is get a definition of being a man that coincides with God's definition of what it means to be a man. And to do that, it's helpful to understand our goal.

That Time Jesus Loaned You A Thousand Bucks

Something we admire, even if we don't realize it, is when a man is able to set a goal, and reach that goal. We're very goal-driven as men. It's just how you're wired. So it's going to be helpful to take a look at what our goal is as a man of God. Because you probably don't want to know a definition. You probably want to know what you're supposed to do with it. So let's start with the goal. And to do that, we should go to the man himself.

Jesus makes it pretty clear what our goal is as a man of God. In Mathew chapter 25 He tells a story to a group of people that helps us understand this a little better. Basically, the story goes something like this:

There was this rich guy who decided he was going to go away for a while. But when you're rich, you can pay people to make you money while you're away. So that's what this guy was going to do. He got three guys that worked for him together and said, "Look guys, I'm going away for a while. So I'm going to leave each of you some money. And while I'm gone, I want you to invest it and turn it into more money for me." Pretty cool gig.

So he gave these guys some money. He gave the first guy $10,000, the second guy $5,000, and the third guy $1,000. And then he goes on his trip. So the guys have decisions to make. The first guy and the second guy each run off immediately and start investing the money. But the third guy was scared. He thought he might lose the money if he invested it poorly. So he dug a hole and put the money in it.

Eventually this rich guy comes back from his trip and wants to hear from the guys he hired. He gets them together and basically says, "What did you do with my money?" The first guy, who had the 10 grand, had doubled his money. So the rich guy is pumped! And he uses this amazing phrase in verse 23;

"Well done good and faithful servant. You have been faithful with a few things; I will put you in charge of many things. Come and share your master's happiness!"

Then the second guy reports that he also doubled his money. And the rich guy again replies,

"Well done good and faithful servant."

But, then the third guy comes up and tells his boss about how he just buried the money and didn't do anything with it. He wasted his time. So the rich guy fires him and gives the thousand to the first guy.

Here's the point of the story. God has given you some money. It's not real money, but he has given you things that you're responsible for. He's given you talents, and abilities, and people to care for, and a lot of opportunities to show Christ's love. And eventually, he's going to look at you and say, "What did you do with my money?" Essentially, God is going to ask you if you used what he gave you well. And your goal at that point is to hear:

Well done. Good and faithful servant.

Everything you do in your life is pointing you towards that goal.

You Got Served

So if that's our goal, what does that tell us about what it means to be a man in God's eyes? I've already said that it has nothing to do with the size of your truck or your biceps. Looking at our goal, a good starting point for our definition of being a man is this:

A real man, is a man who serves God relentlessly.

Let's unpack that a little bit.

"Well done, good and faithful servant" is our goal. Did you notice a weird word in there? Maybe the word servant? As a man, you don't probably like to think of yourself as a servant. Right? You want to be the guy getting fed grapes by the servant. Not the butler answering the door. You want to be the man! We like to think of ourselves as the boss. As the guy who kicks down doors, commands others, and saves the day. Not the servant of that guy.

But that's not what Jesus says. He says we are his servants. He's the big guy. He's the boss. He's the one that left us with a bunch of talents and abilities and expects us to turn them into more glory for Him. Not for us. So, a big step in this is going to be understanding that we are God's servants. Which doesn't feel very manly. But in God's eyes, is the manliest thing you can be.

The Big Picture, Like, The Really Big Picture

In order to be successful in this journey we're going to adopt a new way of thinking. We're going to start thinking "Big Picture." So, what does that mean? Basically, what it means is that we are going to start looking at things with a bigger perspective. Not helpful? Let's look at it this way.

Thinking big picture means keeping your end goal in mind at all times.

It means every decision you make needs to answer the question, "Does this help me reach my end goal?" Little decisions, big decisions, day-to-day decisions, everything now goes through the filter of whether or not it is bringing you closer to your goal, or further from your goal.

So when you're deciding whether to scream at the person in front of you in traffic, would that bring you closer to your goal? When you forget your gym bag at home and want to yell and curse, is that bringing you closer to your goal? When you're alone with your new girlfriend on a Friday night, what decisions will you make to grow closer to your end goal? When a friend needs your help but it's inconvenient, will it bring you closer to your goal?

Everything we do now, from here on out, has to answer the question: *Am I being the best servant of Christ I can be right now?* So with that mentality in mind, I'm going to share with you my definition of what it means to be a man of God. What it means to be manly for us as Christian men. Here it is:

A real man is a man who serves God relentlessly. He constantly has his eyes on the end goal of investing the gifts he's been given to advance God's glory on earth. He is all in, he is unashamed, he is bold, he produces change, and he shows Christ's love through his actions.

The Dotted Line

So we have a working definition of what it means to be a man in God's eyes. We found this definition by looking at our goal in life. Now it's time to get serious. It's time to commit to this goal. One of the first steps in accomplishing any goal is stating it clearly, and committing to it. That's what I want you to do now.

You have to decide if this is your goal. And if you're a Christian man desiring to pursue Christ, it should be. And you need to commit to this goal with everything in you. Sometimes, it's going to be really hard to keep your goal in mind. Sometimes, the world is going to throw a lot of things that seem more important in the moment in front of you, and you might lose sight of it. But you need to commit to this goal first.

Believe me when I say to you that no other goal in your life will be more worth pursuing than this one. Pursuing this goal has challenges. It's going to be tough. But it's the only goal that is truly fulfilling. Pursuing this goal is your life's purpose. And you will never, I promise you, never regret chasing after it with everything in you.

Check out these action steps, and then let's dive into the next chapter.

Action Steps

I've said that the goal is to hear, "Well done good and faithful servant" at the end of our lives. But we can expand on that a little further. Write down how you would define the goal for your life. Here's my example:

> *The goal of my life is to use the gifts, talents, and abilities that God has given me to serve him in everything I do. It is to show the love of Christ to the people I encounter, and to be his light in this world. My goal is to make every decision I make an effort to further God's work on this earth.*

Now you try. It doesn't have to be long. And it doesn't have to be pretty. What's your goal?

_____

_____

_____

What is your new definition of being a man?

_____

_____

_____

This is a serious commitment you're making. You're dedicating the rest of your life to serving your God. Like I said, it's the most fulfilling commitment you can make in your life, but it's a commitment. I want you to take some time to really think about what you are committing to. And then when you're ready, sign below indicating that you're all in. That you're committed to your goal, and you are going to start chasing it.

Signature_____

Name_____ Date _____

KNOW WHAT YOU KNOW

Seven-Year-Old Thinking

When I was seven years old, I thought a lot of crazy things were true.

I thought girls were yucky

I thought the tooth fairy existed

I thought winter was the best season

I thought I was a San-Francisco 49ers fan

I thought I was going to play professional baseball

But I also wanted to drive a UPS truck

I thought there were monsters at the end of my bed, so I slept with my legs tucked to my chest

I thought I would never get married

I thought spiders could crawl out of the toilet and get you when you were seated

I thought wearing a helmet on my bike was dumb

I thought drinking and driving meant you couldn't have a Coke in the car

Some of them are a little crazier than others, but I honestly believed all of them.

Seven is also the time in my life when I was first introduced to the idea of Jesus. It was the first time I said my little prayer consisting of something like, "Dear Jesus, please come into my heart." With no understanding of what that meant, what my end of the deal was, or why I was doing it. But around seven, I said this prayer.

After saying this prayer, I was taught a lot of things that I believed. A lot of you probably had a similar experience. You went to church. Your parents, or grandparents, or some close adult, instructed you about who God is, and that became your belief system. That's how it worked for me. So at seven years old, I knew everything I needed to know about God, Jesus, and the Bible. I knew what I believed.

But let's take a look at some of the other things I believed at seven. What if I hadn't rethought some of those ideas when I was a teenager? Do you know the kinds of nicknames a guy can get for believing in the tooth fairy in 11th grade? What if I had never realized the infinite superiority of the Pittsburgh Steelers to every other team? What if I still thought girls were yucky? Or what if I still thought there were monsters at the end of my bed?

Can you imagine what life would be like for me if I had never thought to adjust what I believed about these issues? Luckily in most areas of our life we're encouraged to continually adapt our belief system. So I eventually learned that I'm not nearly athletic enough to play baseball professionally. I learned the hard way that wearing a helmet is not dumb. And after careful consideration, I realized that fall is way better than winter. I rethought what I believed. And so did you. (If you just now learned that there is no tooth fairy… I'm so sorry you had to find out this way).

Isn't it interesting that one of the only things we're not encouraged to rethink is what we believe about God? Isn't it strange that we would never consider believing the same thing about Santa at seven and seventeen, but we're perfectly comfortable never questioning what we believe about God? A lot of you reading this right now have never really thought about what you believe. And I think it's time we get started.

The Big Question

One of the most important questions anyone can ever ask you in your life is: *Why do you believe what you believe?*

Why do you believe what you believe? For the most part, the church, youth groups, and parents, are not asking you this question. Most of the time we're too busy telling you what you believe, not why you believe it. This is a question I didn't get asked until I was well into college. And I wish I'd been asked earlier.

Because here's the thing, what you believe is important. You could make the argument that what you believe, is who you are. And what you believe about God, is drastically important. You're a man now, and as a man, you're going to make decisions. You're going to decide to do things, or not to do them. And what you decide to do is going to be directly impacted by what you believe.

Here's an example. Let's suppose you're at the beach. Sand, ocean, sun, fun. But let's imagine you think there's a shark in the water. You believe there is a shark in the water. Maybe someone told you there was, maybe you saw something that looked like a fin, it doesn't matter. You believe there is a shark in the water. Is this belief going to impact your decisions? Of course it is! You're not going in that water! But not only that, you're going to stop other people from going into that water. You're not just going to sit by and watch a happy family wade into the ocean when you think there's a shark in there! You're going to be yelling and running and waving your arms to get them out of there.

It's the same way with your beliefs about God. If you believe God is forgiving and has forgiven you, you're going to be more forgiving to others. If you think God is vengeful, you're probably going to seek vengeance. If you think Jesus loved the poor, you might be interested in volunteering with the homeless. But if you think God is punishing the homeless, you probably won't. I could go on and on, but I think it's clear that what you believe, shapes everything you do. And what could be more important than what you believe about God?

What you believe about God will impact every decision you make in your life. And because of this, it's super important that we take some time to answer the question: why do you believe what you believe? What you believe about God is too important to let someone else decide for you. You need to know what you believe, and that that belief is yours.

Tracking Down The Beginning

So when I was in college, I decided I needed to know what I believed, and why I believed it. So I started on this journey to figure out why I believed what I believed. And in order to do that, I found that I needed to go all the way back to when

I started having these beliefs. The process looked something like this:

I would start with a belief that I had. It doesn't really matter what it was. Maybe it was "Noah built the ark to save the world from a flood." Pretty common belief amongst church attendees. So I started with that and I asked, "Why do I believe that?" Why do I believe that Noah built an ark?

I thought about it and decided that I believed Noah built the ark because it said so in the Bible. "The Bible tells me so!" Perfect. That was why I had that belief. But it turns out I wasn't quite done. This didn't really answer my question. What it did was introduce me to another belief that I had to track down. Now I needed to know why I thought the Bible was right. So I kept going. "Why do I believe that the Bible is true?"

When I thought about this one, I realized that I'd been told that the Bible was true by a lot of people in my life. My Sunday school teacher had told me this, my school teacher at the Christian school I attended had told me this, my pastor had told me this… I had heard this from many different sources. So I kept going. "Why do I believe these people?"

When I got to the bottom of it, I realized that the only reason I knew and trusted any of these people was because of my parents. My parents had taken me to church, put me in school, and helped to teach me everything I knew. I realized that I believed everything I believed because of my parents. This was my answer to why I believed what I believed. My parents had told me. Everything I believed about God, Jesus, the Bible, all of it, had been handed to me by my parents.

Your story might look similar to mine, or it might have gone very differently, but in the end, you probably believe what you believe because someone told you to believe it. This person or people were probably trustworthy and had great intentions. But much like I needed to rethink what I believed when I was seven, you need to know for yourself what you believe. Not what someone else told you to believe.

My parents were a trustworthy source, *but I still needed to think it through for myself.* And you need to do the same thing. You can do this by building on what you already believe, and challenging it to make it your own. I'm not asking you to walk away from your beliefs, I'm not calling your parents liars, I just want you to know that what you believe as your own. Your beliefs need to be *yours.*

What your parents or pastor or whoever told you might be great. It might be exactly what you believe as well. But you need to know for yourself. Too many men are walking around today with the same belief system they had when they were seven just because they never took the time to wonder if it was what *they* believed. They've never thought it through for themselves. We don't need any more men that can recite Sunday school answers. We need men that have done the work, challenged what they believe, and claimed it for their own. Only then are men truly ready to make decisions for the glory of God. And I want you to get an early start.

How To Hold Your Faith Like Your Phone

Pick up your phone. What am I talking about, you're already holding it. Even as you're reading this book, you're probably still holding your phone. If not, pick it up. Now, notice how you're holding your phone. We never think about holding our phone, because holding it has become as second nature as blinking. But let's think about it for a minute.

How are you holding it? What's your grip like? My guess is it's perfect. Unless you're reading this on top of a waterfall, or in a hot air balloon or something, you're probably not crushing it in your hand. You're probably not squeezing it intentionally for fear that it will be taken from you. You're probably not breaking that Otterbox or warping it into an odd "C" shaped phone device.

But if somebody bumped into you, you probably wouldn't drop it either. You probably don't have it resting on your open palm held above your head like a fresh pizza pie. An aggressive breeze wouldn't remove it from your hand. You're not crushing it, but you're not going to drop it either.

This is how your beliefs about God need to work as well. You're not crushing them to death, but you're not going to drop them either. There are some beliefs in your life that you're going to hold onto tightly. There are some questions that you'll have answers to, and you're going to hold onto them with a firm grip. But there are other beliefs in your life that are going to grow with you. They'll come into your life, but you'll eventually let them go.

You know what you believe, but you also have the understanding that *as you grow, so will your belief system.* There's a real lack of men who have grasped this concept. So many men are walking around, crushing their beliefs in their Kung-fu death grip. Nothing can ever be changed, nothing can get in, and nothing can get out. And many others are walking around just letting their faith fall out of their hand. Every new idea changes everything about who they are, and nothing ever gets built firmly.

Getting Started

You're a man of God. And as such, you need to start wrestling with what you believe and why you believe it. If you start thinking about it now, you'll be ahead of the game when college, and adult life come around. Sometimes, this process can seem scary, and can even feel like you're betraying what you believe, and the people that taught you to believe it. But believe me, if you take the time to think through your beliefs for yourself, you'll be able to tell people what you believe, you'll be able to make decisions with more confidence, and you'll grow in your relationship with Christ exponentially. Check out these action steps, and let's keep moving.

Action Steps

Your action steps for this chapter are to start thinking about your faith for yourself. Here are five questions that I think are critical to have an understanding of in your walk with Christ. Really take your time with these, and try to avoid what I call "Sunday school answers." Think it through like it's the first time you've ever been asked the question, and try to figure out what YOU believe about these questions. Use the examples I gave above to help you with the process.

What is the Bible? Why do you believe that?

_____

_____

_____

_____

Who is Jesus? Why do you believe that?

_____

_____

_____

_____

Why did Jesus die on the cross?

_____

_____

_____

_____

What is our purpose on earth?

_____

_____

_____

_____

What happens when we die?

_____

_____

_____

_____

Those should get you started. Now, what are some other beliefs that you need to think through for yourself? Try to list three, and what you believe about them.

1) _____

_____

_____

2) _____

_____

_____

3) _____

_____

_____

FOCUS UP

Your Imaginary Girlfriend

I want you to imagine you have a girlfriend. I know, for some of you that's a bit of a stretch, but imagine she exists. And she wants to be with you. So let's imagine in your relationship you only see her once per week for like an hour. And the whole time you're talking to her, you keep checking the clock, and you keep getting distracted while you're with her, and you complain the whole time that you have to spend time with her. You avoid talking about her at school, and if someone asks you about her, you say you don't know her. You only call her when something has gone wrong, or you need someone to blame for a mistake you've made. And most of the time you just completely ignore her.

Now. Tell me. Is she going to stay with you very long?

Hopefully not. You're not investing in the relationship. It's completely one-sided, and borderline abusive. She should leave you. We would never expect a relationship like this to last.

But for some reason, we're completely comfortable with our relationship with God looking exactly like that. We watch the clock through church to make sure we make kickoff, we never pray, we don't talk about God with our friends, and we blame Him for our mistakes. We're pursuing a *relationship* with Christ. And if we're going to do that, we need to be investing in that relationship daily.

Not Again...

I know what you're thinking. Oh great. Another guy that's going to tell me to pray and read my Bible. Well, yeah, sort of. But in a different way. Maybe you're like I was and you've tried this before. I remember when I was around seventeen, I decided to get serious about my relationship with Christ. So I decided I was going to read my Bible every night before I went to bed. So I did what any logical person would do. I started at the beginning of the book and just started reading it. Well, I got about half way through the book of Leviticus, which is only like page 50, and quit right there.

People had been telling me I needed to have a quiet time, that I should be praying and reading my Bible, but they never told me how to do it. They never told me how to get the most out of it, or that I would eventually look forward to my quiet time with God. But they also never told me just how important and life-changing it could be. So we're going to start with that, why it's so important and the change you'll see in your life from it. Then we'll look at some strategies for your quiet time and some practical ways to get it started.

Claiming It

Okay, so much like the imaginary relationship we talked about to start this chapter, your relationship with Christ is going to take some work. But there's nothing in the world worth pursuing more that this relationship. And one of the biggest ways to grow this relationship is by having a time set aside, every day, only to work on this relationship. Think about it. When you want to pursue something you work at it every day. If you want bigger biceps, you should be hitting hammer curls in the gym every day. If you want to play basketball, you need to be practicing layups every day. If you want to make the chess team, you need to be studying opening strategies. And if you want a relationship with Christ, you need to dig in every day.

Some people call this doing your devotions or "Devos" for short. I don't really like this word. Devotions sounds like an obligation. It sounds like something you have to do. It's like it's how we show people how devoted we are. Or that we're trying to prove something to God. I like to call it my Focus Time.

F.O.C.U.S. Frequently Obtaining Christ frUm Silence.

Ok, it's a terrible acronym. But it only took me five seconds to make it up. You don't need an acronym. But maybe something like devotions or quiet time doesn't really work for you. I never really liked the phrase quiet time, because that sounds boring and tedious. So, that's why I call it a focus time.

When you think of focus time, I want you to think of the ten minutes in the locker room before the big game. Where you sit in silence on the bench focusing on your goal. You can already hear the crowd cheering. Other players are nervous and jittery around you. But you are intentionally focusing on your goal. That's what I mean by focus time. It's a time set aside to do nothing but focus on your goal and grow in your relationship with Christ.

For Real, It's Worth It

So, we kind of rebranded quiet time into focus time. Now, what's the point? Well, let's look at a few benefits of having a focus time before moving into anything more specific.

Knowing God More

The first advantage of having a focus time every day is that it helps you to know God more. I've already discussed in an earlier chapter that it's important to know what you believe. And one of the ways you gain this is by having a daily time where you are actively trying to get to know God better. When you get into the Bible, you start to see new attributes about God that you didn't know before. When you start to pray more, you realize how easy it is to talk to God. When you have time set aside, just to listen to what God is trying to say to you, you might be surprised by what you hear. There's always more to find out about God. Always. Part of having a focus time is learning everything you can.

Fighting Off Temptation

So, you've probably heard of the devil, or Satan, or "the enemy of our souls." I usually just call him the devil. However you envision evil, here's the thing about it. The devil has no power over you. For real. He has no power over you whatsoever. The devil's only power is that of temptation. And one of the benefits of having a focus time is that it helps you fight off temptation. Focusing on the Bible and God every day helps you to recognize temptation, and to avoid it.

The thing about temptation is that it's always a matter of distracting you from your goal. It's so easy to forget what we're trying to do when we're being tempted. You remember your goal right? Does "Well done good and faithful servant" ring a bell? But we forget what we actually want. We forget how much happier we are when we're pursuing Christ instead of temptation. But when you have a focus time every day you can do exactly that. You can focus on your goal. You can set your sights on it and not get distracted when temptation enters your life.

Gaining Clarity

You're in an interesting time in life. A lot of things are constantly changing, and the future isn't very clear. Having a focus time in your life gives you the chance to listen to God. I'm going to give you some relationship advice. It applies to your focus time, but it also applies to your relationships with people. You need to listen more than you speak. Not always. But when the other person is talking, you need to listen, and not worry about what you are going to say. God is always trying to speak to you. *Always.* Sometimes, we don't hear because we're too busy talking.

If you incorporate a time of listening into your focus time, you will gain tremendous clarity. God will tell you what He wants you to do next. He will tell you when you shouldn't do something. God is speaking to you. And we can have great clarity in our lives if we have time set aside to listen.

Feeling Recharged

Having a focus time recharges you. It brings peace to your life. When you spend time with God every day, it's hard to feel overwhelmed by the world. When you've spent time speaking with and hanging out with the creator of the world... all of a sudden you don't feel so stressed. You don't feel so tired. You know why you were created, and that you have the God of the universe in your corner. You feel recharged and ready for anything.

I could go on for a while with the benefits, but hopefully these have piqued your interest. You'll discover more benefits as you get started with this.

Excuses, Excuses, Excuses

"But Andy. You don't understand. I don't have time, and I get so bored, and I always fall asleep, and I get distracted, and me and God are good, I'm just not into the quiet time thing..." Yeah. I know. You got ninety-nine reasons why you can't have a focus time every day. I've told you some of the benefits. Now let me remind you that Jesus modeled this for us. Time and time again throughout His life we see Jesus going off on His own to pray. Jesus had a focus time. And He was Jesus. He had more stress, less time, and more to get done than you do. So let's take a look at how this can work for you.

Maybe you feel like you don't have enough time to fit a focus time in every day. Yes you do. There, that was easy! Yes you do. If you watch any television, you have time for a focus time. If you spend any time on YouTube, you have time. If you spend time just kind of opening the refrigerator to see if anything appeared, you have time. I think you get my point. You can find time in your day to focus. Maybe it's first thing in the morning. Maybe right after school. Maybe it's that time between school and practice. Maybe right before bed. You can find time.

And I know you can because it doesn't have to take long. In fact, I'm going to encourage you to start small. Don't start out by trying to read the Bible for half an hour; pray for half an hour, and have ten minutes of meditation. You're going to burn out quickly. I like the **five and five rule.** Read your Bible for five minutes. Then pray for five minutes. And then you can go on YouTube to your heart's content.

Here are a few pointers with the five and five rule. For one, it doesn't have to be five and five. It can be two and two if you need it to be when you start out. Or 30 seconds and 30 seconds. It doesn't matter. Just get started. I promise you'll want more once you start doing this.

Second, don't start at the beginning of the Bible. Starting at the beginning sounds logical right? But the Bible doesn't really read like other books. It has different sections, with different characters at different times, with very different content. And the beginning is actually one of the trickiest, and, dare I say it, more boring sections of the Bible. Start with one of the gospels (Mathew, Mark, Luke, or John). They tell the story of Jesus and His teachings. They're a great place to get started.

Third, don't set a timer or anything. Just find what works for you. If you can read for a few minutes, then pray for a few minutes each day, you'll see changes in your life. And you'll start to crave more. A timer starts to feel like an obligation. Your focus time is for your benefit. If you're not enjoying it, or find yourself watching the clock, make some changes.

Finally, don't get upset when you find that you can't focus during your focus time. Ironic right? You'll probably find that you sit down to pray, and start thinking about something else moments into your focus time. That's okay. It takes practice.

Your brain isn't used to slowing down and focusing. It's been trained to run at 100 miles per hour all the time. Give it some time, and don't get discouraged. Soon, you'll be able to focus without getting distracted.

Don't Feel Locked In

One final thing I want to say about your focus time. You need to make it yours, and you need to feel free to do what you need to do. Maybe some days, you need to just walk in the woods and listen to God. (That's one of my personal favorites). Maybe for you— it's dancing in your room as worship. Maybe you want to play your guitar and sing some worship songs. Maybe you want to watch a preacher online. Maybe you want to use a devotional app. Maybe you need to watch worship videos on YouTube. You don't have to feel locked into the five and five model. I want you to be praying and reading your Bible. But not if it's become an obligation. *The point is to connect with God every day.*

As long as you're doing that consistently, it doesn't really matter how you do it. The point isn't to check "Focus Time" off your to-do list. The point is to have a time every day when you're actively pursuing your relationship with God. I hope you'll start finding the time to focus every day.

Fill out the action steps for this chapter. Then let's keep rolling.

Action Steps

What time can you have a focus time every day? Be specific. What time, where?

_____

_____

_____

_____

What are the reasons you don't have a focus time? And are these just excuses?

_____

_____

_____

_____

What is your focus time going to look like? Be specific. (Will you use a guide? Will you be using the five and five model? What section of the Bible will you start with?...)

_____

_____

_____

_____

What are some benefits you have seen from having a focus time?

_____

_____

_____

_____

YOUR PRICE TAG

Hi! How Do You Value Yourself?

So there's this crazy phenomenon that happens in society today. When you meet someone for the first time, what's usually the first question you ask them? If you're like me, you tell them your name and ask for theirs.

"Hi, my name's Andy. What's yours?"

"My name is Sean."

So far so good. That's not the interesting part. The interesting part to me is that almost every one of us would ask the same second question.

"Nice to meet you Sean. *What do you do?*"

Maybe this isn't exactly how you start conversations in high school. It's probably something like,

Are you taking a language this year?

Do you play any sports?

Are you in a band?

But in the end, we're still asking, "What do you do?"

As a society, we're obsessed with this question. We spend our entire lives fixating on what we do. And this is especially true for men. As men we gain a huge part of our identity from what we do. You may identify as a soccer player. Or maybe you're the first chair clarinet. Or maybe you're a poet. Maybe you would call yourself a good student, or an athlete, or a nerd (which I understand is no longer an insult?) but you've probably assigned part of your identity to what you do. That's okay. Society has taught us to do that, and we all fall prey to it from time to time. The problem starts when we take it to the next level.

Taking It Too Far

As a society, we not only find part of our identity from what we do, we also find our value from what we do.

We have bought into the lie that value equals achievement. You're only as valuable as what you've accomplished. You're only worth what you've been able to do. That's why you see guys that make millions of dollars working sleepless nights to make billions. That's why you see guys at the gym trying to beat personal bests. That's why we have to drive the fastest car, have the hottest girl, and wear the sharpest suits. We've decided that our value comes from our accomplishments. What we do equals what we're worth.

So, in the matter of one short conversation, we've gone from "This is who I am"

To "This is what I do"

To "This is what I'm worth"

Essentially, we're saying "This is why I'm valuable." As men, this is a very easy trap to fall into. And it's a dangerous one for several reasons. For one thing, if we believe our value comes from our accomplishments, we'll never be satisfied. Enough will never be enough. We'll be driven to be better, but for all of the wrong reasons, because accomplishments and achievements will have become so much more than they were meant to be. If we're pursuing value with accomplishments, we can never stop.

In addition to that, if your value is based on your accomplishments, it can only ever be temporary. A value based on achievement is impermanent; it's subject to change. What happens when you hit a losing streak? What happens when you get cut or fired? What if you get injured and can't throw touchdowns? What if you lose interest and want to pursue something else? If you're not accomplishing, don't you still have value? Your value isn't dependent on anything. But when you place your value on accomplishments, you start to feel like you can lose your value.

The Real Question At Hand

So if we're discussing where we find our value as men, we need to look at what the root question is. We do all of these things to prove our value. We make money, buy stuff, get girls, chop wood, grow beards, all to prove that we have some value. But at the end of the day what we're really getting at is trying to find out the answer to this all-important question:

Am I a man?

"Am I a man?" has kept more men awake at night than any horror movie, loud noise, or small bladder ever could. It's the big question we're all asking, and trying desperately to find out. Because if we're not a man, do we have any value?

High school can make this question especially difficult. Suddenly you find yourself in high school. You are a man. But you have no idea if you *are* a man because you got cut from the football team. You know you could get the lead in the school musical, and you really want to, but would you be a man then? Also, you're not that great at math. Which, I guess is the manliest of the core academia. But you are good at English. You like to read, but nothing with pictures of cars or women, which are the manliest of reading materials. You don't have big muscles, you don't know who Tom Brady is, and you drive your mom's old minivan to school, which, ironically enough, because it was designed for families, is the least manly vehicle known to mankind. Suddenly, society is screaming from every angle, "You are not a man!" And you believe it.

Or maybe the opposite is true for you. You're the football captain. Or you're the lead guitar in your band. Or maybe you're the valedictorian of your high school. Maybe you do have a lot of accomplishments. Maybe you do have a lot of the attributes that society associates with a man like muscles, a cool car, athleticism, and a beard. But you still lay awake at night wondering if it's enough. You still doubt your value. You still obsess over your failures. And you're constantly afraid that your value could be taken from you.

We've already talked fairly extensively about the need to redefine what it means to be a man. But all of that had to do with what we do as men. This is going much deeper. This question burns well past what we do and goes deep into the realm of who we are. This question, "Am I a man?" really sums up all that we are trying to know as men. "Who am I?" and "Do I have any value?"

So let's talk about where your value really comes from, and if you have any.

Being Valued

Let's look at the bigger picture here. It's possible that Sandwich Joe doesn't think you're a man because you can't eat a three foot-hoagie. And it's possible that Deltoid Dan bases his self-worth, and yours, on how much he deadlifts. And you may not earn the respect of Bill "The Beard" Bunyon. But does that really matter? Let's review, whose approval are we trying to gain? Who are we trying to hear "Well done good and faithful servant" from? Oh that's right, God.

So let's jump straight to the part that matters. Joe, Dan, and Bill can judge as much as they like. Let's take a look at how God sees our value. I think one of the most important ideas for us to understand in the Bible is found in 1 Corinthians, and its verses 19-20a. It reads:

> *Don't you realize that your body is the temple of the Holy Spirit, who lives in you and was given to you by God? You do not belong to yourself, for God bought you with a high price.*

Did you catch that? What did God buy you for? *A high price.* A high price is something we assign to something with value.

You don't put a high price on junk. You don't put a high price on something artificial. You only pay a high price for something that has value.

Let me make something very clear to you. Your value does not come from what you do, or have accomplished. Your value comes from being loved by a God who has said you are valuable. Your value comes from being created by a God who decided to create you. You were created by a God who doesn't make junk. You are loved by the only one whose opinion matters. God loves you. God is in you. *You have value because God assigned you value.*

So yes. You have value. And yes. You are a man.

God created you exactly as you are. *On Purpose.* God knew that he was going to need a man exactly like you, with your skills, abilities, knowledge, and gifts. Regardless of what the world has to say about those skills, abilities, knowledge and gifts. God looked down and said, "I need a man," and He created you. Just by being created by our God intentionally lets you know without a doubt that you are a man. You are a man in God's eyes.

God paid a high price to have you. He didn't have to. He could have left you with no value. He could have decided not to purchase you. But He didn't. He paid a high price for you. And that price was Jesus. Maybe you've heard John 3:16 before. It's one of the most well-known verses in the Bible. It's also one of the most consistently underappreciated verses in the Bible. Check this out. John 3:16 reads,

> *For this is how God loved the world: He gave his one and only Son, so that everyone who believes in him will not perish but have eternal life.*

We learn this one as children. And we read it the same way for the rest of our lives. "Yup, God so loved the world. Everybody knows that." But think about what this is saying. God looked at you and thought about your value. He considered your worth. God looked down at *you*. With all of your struggles. All of your pain. All of your shortcomings. All of your flaws. And thought about what price He would be willing to pay for you.

And He decided that you were worth so much, you had so much value, and you were so much of a man that you were worth the death of His son. *You were worth it.* God looked at you and placed a high price on you. And paid it.

This is how I know you have value. This is how I know you're a real man. Because God said so. God paid a high, high, high price for you. Jesus' death and suffering. God doesn't make junk. And God doesn't purchase junk. You've been assigned a high value, just by being created as you are.

Forgetting Our Value

Now, I get it. "Yeah Yeah, God loves me, I'm a real man, great." It probably doesn't make you feel better about getting cut from the wrestling team. It probably doesn't help you with your lack of large muscles. It probably doesn't make you feel like more of a man. This one's tough.

It's tough because you're still in the habit of placing your value on your accomplishments. You're still thinking about performance based manhood. And it's a tough habit to break. Everything in society and even church tells you that performance is where your value is earned. And you're going to have to work through that before any of this is helpful. Luckily, you're getting an early start. If you can master this one early, it will put you ahead in life in so many ways.

Suddenly you don't have to do things to keep your value. Can you imagine that? Can you imagine feeling like a man, knowing that you're a real man with value and worth, even if you fail? Even if you come up short of your goals? What would it be like if you knew your value regardless of if you were successful or not? Because the truth is, even if you reach all of your goals, you'll still be asking the question, "Am I a man?" until you realize that your value never came from your accomplishments. It came from being assigned a high price from your Creator.

Check out these action steps, and let's keep rolling.

Action Steps

What are some ways you have been trying to earn your value?

_____

_____

_____

_____

Why don't accomplishments cause us to feel more valuable?

_____

_____

_____

_____

What are some risks of placing your value in your accomplishments?

_____

_____

_____

_____

Take a few minutes to write out why you are valuable.

_____

_____

_____

_____

DATING 101

I'm tryna find the words to describe
this girl without being disrespectful...
*D*** you'se a sexy b*****

Permanent Handprint

Ahh... poetry. The above lyrics come from a song written and performed by David Guetta featuring Akon. A modern day love sonnet if you will.

And that's exactly the problem. The way talking to girls goes these days; it's a wonder more guys don't have permanent hand prints indented across their faces. When it comes to dating, society hasn't set the bar very high. Especially in high school. So let's talk about dating, and what it looks like in a Christian man's life.

Prepped

Much like you're preparing for everything else in your life at this stage, you can now begin prepping for dating. This is a great time for you to create some healthy habits and approaches to dating that will apply now and for the rest of your life.

Society is doing a really poor job with the way we're supposed to pursue women, talk to girls, date, have relationships, all of it. As a Christian man, people should be able to see a difference in the way you date girls in high school, and after you graduate. You should be representing Christ in your relationships the same way you do in every other aspect of your life.

So if you decide that you're going to date in high school, or even middle school, we need to talk about some ways that your relationship is going to look differently from the rest of the world's relationships. Let's talk about how you can SCORE.

S.C.O.R.E.

Yes. I know what it means to score in a relationship. I played a lot of sports growing up, so I spent a lot of time in locker rooms. I know what it means. But in sports scoring is a good thing. It's your goal really. Whoever scores the most wins. So I want to look at a new way of thinking about scoring in dating. What does it mean to S.C.O.R.E. you ask?

S.piritualize

C.hivalry

O.pen spaces

R.elease the pressure

E.valuate

Spiritualize

I don't know if that's a real word or not. But I like it. It means bringing spirituality to your relationship. You need to be intentionally talking about God in your relationship. You need to have practices put in place that are going to bring you closer to God. *The true purpose of a relationship is to bring each other closer to God.* The only way a girl should be able to get closer to you is by getting closer to God. So you need to have a real spiritual component to your relationship.

This will look different for every relationship, and there aren't any rules about what needs to be in place. But things like praying for each other and with each other will go a long way. If you can go to church together, go to church together. Talk about what God is doing in your lives with each other. Maybe even read through a devotional together. Just find a few ways that you're intentionally making Christ the center of your relationship.

This will set your relationship apart from the rest of the world and will help the two of you grow together towards Christ. This functions the same way as having your own focus time in your personal life does. If you're both plugging in and recharging and refocusing, you'll be able to keep your relationship Christ-centered, fight off temptation, and know how to progress together.

Chivalry

Chivalry is an old word that we don't use very often anymore. It originally referred to the code by which knights were supposed to live by, but in our modern culture it has basically come to mean being a gentleman. We don't settle things with swords and shields anymore, but a chivalrous man is still respectful, cares for others, seeks justice, and looks out for the betterment of others. It was a code of honor.

I'm not suggesting you start riding a horse or try to slay a dragon. But I am suggesting you open the door for her when you get to the restaurant. I am saying you should walk up to her door when you pick her up. Don't just blow the horn from the street. Walk up, meet her dad, and shake his hand. Remember her birthday. Never say anything negative about her to your friends. If there's a problem, talk to her, not about her to other people. Buy her a card or flowers if you have some extra cash. Give her a compliment. Write her a letter. Go out of your way to be respectful and courteous.

Things like this are rarely seen today. This has several effects. For one, it shows that you genuinely care about this girl. You wouldn't go out of your way to do these things if you didn't, and that shows her that you care. It shows her that she deserves to be treated well and that you understand that. She gets special treatment because she is special to you. But it also shows her and others that there is something different about you. It's one small way you can represent Christ in your relationships.

Open Spaces

Open spaces basically means dating in public. And dating in public means never being alone. Now, of course you need to spend time alone. You need to get to know each other, and have important conversations, and these need to happen with just the two of you. But where you have these conversations doesn't have to be private. And I'm going to argue that they shouldn't be.

I heard a funny quote on a TV show once where a father was letting his daughter go to a party. And as she walked out the door, he yelled, "God sees everything you do! Even in the dark!"

I thought it was a really funny way of communicating the importance of this third letter in SCORE. There are so many temptations that come from being completely alone. Just knowing that you could get away with something makes you want to do it. Privacy by itself is enough to give your brain the extra hit of hormones it needs to completely forget all of your rules, goals, and boundaries. If you want to be sure you're honoring God in your relationship, you need to be seeking open spaces.

Plus, it's super easy to do. Going to a movie is an open space. Yes, it's dark, but there are people around. Going to the park is an open space. Ice skating is an open space. Your parents' house is an open space. Your church youth group is an open space. A group hang creates an open space. The reality is, *you don't need privacy if you're not doing anything inappropriate.* If you're honoring God, it shouldn't matter if someone walks in on you. Seek open spaces to alleviate the temptation.

Release The Pressure

This next one is absolutely critical. It's one of the most important things you can do when you're dating, and it's one of the hardest to follow up on. As a man of God it is your responsibility to set boundaries in your relationship. I've already argued that finding open spaces should be part of your boundaries, but this is taking it a step further. You need to be the one to initiate a conversation where you both set clear physical boundaries for what is permissible in your relationship.

It is critical that you have this conversation early in the relationship, and that you both agree on what is allowed, and what is not. And once you've decided on them, you have to stick to it. *As a man of God you can never pressure her. Ever.* That's what I mean by release the pressure. Once you've established clear and reasonable boundaries, it is your responsibility to make sure you both hold to them. Too often, it's the young man in the relationship who is trying to push the boundaries. This can't happen in your relationships. You are a man of God. And as such, you have a responsibility to uphold the boundaries you've set in your relationship.

The boundaries you set will be unique to every relationship. Some people say it's okay to kiss, some say it's not. You'll need to decide for yourself. But if I could give you some pointers I'd say it's okay to hold hands. It's okay to hug. It's okay to kiss for less than three seconds, and no more often than once per every five minutes, up to five times per night. An arm around the shoulder is okay in an open space but not in a private place. No tongue. No touching above the knee. And don't carry a condom with you "just in case." That mentality says it could happen. **It cannot.** Sex needs to be saved for marriage. It really is a big deal, it really does change things, and it really is worth the wait. (More on this later)

Boundaries need to be set before you find yourself in a situation where they could be pushed. By setting them early, you relieve yourself of the responsibility of trying to think when you're in the moment. If you have them clearly laid out ahead of time, you won't have to think. You'll just know when to stop. Setting boundaries early will let you honor God and her in all situations.

Evaluate

This one is the last one in the list, but it's the first one you need to do. Before you enter into a relationship, you need to evaluate yourself. You need to look at yourself and see if you're really ready to enter into a relationship. Relationships, even in high school, are a big responsibility. You're taking another person's feelings, emotions, and trust into your hands. And you need to decide if you're ready to do that.

A good place to start is asking yourself why you want to date. There are a lot of reasons people decide to start dating, some of them are good, and some of them are not so good. Are you trying to date girls just because it looks fun? Or just because everyone seems to be trying to date? Is it a matter of status? Do you think it proves your masculinity or makes you look cool to have a girl? Are you just trying to hook up with someone? Or are you genuinely looking for a potential lifelong partner?

Look, the truth is, some of you need to make a conscious decision not to date right now. Maybe you still need to figure out some things you believe before you can lead a relationship. Maybe if you're being honest, you're only dating because you feel inadequate without a girlfriend. Maybe you're trying to get laid. I could go on. But the reality is some of you should wait a while before thinking about dating. This is a good time in life to work on yourself. Make sure you're the man she deserves before you start dating her.

Sisters in Christ

I hope you'll take the SCORE model from above seriously when considering dating or not dating. But whether you decide to date now, later, or never, you need to understand a very important aspect of our relationship with girls. Every one of us is a child of God. God created and claimed every one of you reading this book. We often use the word Father to describe God, which would make us His sons.

God also created and claimed every girl in the world. Every single one. Making them His daughters. The thing about God is, He's a very protective God. Much like fathers on earth, God is protective of His daughters. He wants the best for them. He created each and every one of them uniquely and specially. He gave them dreams, and hopes, and skills, and abilities, and wants the world for them. And yet; sometimes, God's daughters are mistreated by men. Sometimes they are yelled at, manipulated, pressured, or even physically harmed by men.

These are your sisters in Christ. Just as God is protective of them, you need to be protective of your sisters in Christ. You have an obligation as a man of God to treat every girl you meet with absolute respect. You need to treat her like the child of God she is. *Like your sister in Christ.* It is your role to defend them when they are mistreated. And to ensure that they are never disrespected in a relationship of yours.

I don't care who she is. I don't care about her reputation. I don't care what she's done. I don't care what she looks like, how she dresses, how she talks, or anything about her. Simply by being a loved daughter of God, she deserves your respect. And it is your job to care for your sisters in Christ.

I hope you'll take this chapter seriously. I hope you'll really look into if you're ready to be dating at this point. I hope you'll take your job seriously and lead your relationships. And I hope you'll remember your role in respecting and defending your sisters in Christ. Check out the action steps for this chapter. And let's keep moving.

Action Steps

What are some ways you can spiritualize your relationships?

_____

_____

_____

_____

What are some chivalrous actions that you can apply in your relationships? (ie. Buying flowers, not cursing, opening doors...)

_____

_____

_____

_____

What are some open spaces that would allow you privacy, but not temptation that you can think of?

_____

_____

_____

_____

What are some boundaries that you think should to be in place for your relationships?

_____

_____

_____

_____

What are some things you need to change before you start dating?

_____

_____

_____

_____

THE MOST UNCOMFORTABLE CHAPTER EVER

I Know You Don't Want To...

Let's talk about sex! Since we're on the subject. The odds are pretty good that you've never had a conversation with an adult about sex that wasn't completely and totally uncomfortable. Maybe you remember learning where babies come from. Or maybe at some point you've had someone aggressively tell you that sex is bad, and evil, and if you have it you will die. Well, I'd like this chapter to add one more conversation to the list of uncomfortable conversations you've had. Because it's important.

The odds are pretty good that most conversations around this particular topic have been long lists of reasons you should not be having sex.

"You could catch an STD"

"You don't want to get a girl pregnant"

"You're just not ready. Trust me"

"The Bible says so"

And these are actually pretty good reasons. But these might have you feeling a little confused and even trapped. These reasons probably left you with more questions than answers.

"If sex is so bad, and we're supposed to wait for it, then why am I physically ready for sex at this age?

"Why doesn't my desire for sex not kick in until after high school, when I'm thinking about getting married?"

"Why do I feel like such a sexual person, if I'm not supposed to act on it?"

"It seems like everyone is having sex but me! What's the big deal?"

All fair questions. It really doesn't seem fair, and in part, it's not. Just by being a man, you're more prone to lust. It just comes with the territory. You're a man, so you're naturally visually stimulated. Which means when you see an attractive young lady, you find her stimulating. Just looking at a female is enough to start to feel more and more like you're ready. This is natural. It's not your fault

But there's more to it than that. You've also been kind of set up for failure. See, you've been born into a world that has become completely and totally *obsessed* with sex. So, you've spent your entire life being completely pumped full of sexual innuendo, content, humor, images, marketing, clothing, everything. Everywhere you look, sex is just screaming back at you. And because of this, we've made being a Christian young man way more difficult than it has to be. So before we get into sex itself, let's take a look at why you feel so trapped.

Submerged

The world you've inherited isn't your fault. You were born into a society that genuinely and truly believes that sex, is everything. Everything you do is about sex. Everything you buy is about sex. Just think about how we market products today.

We have billboards featuring scantily clad women next to big letters that read, "Buy a new truck!" We tell men to wear this cologne because women will think you smell good, and then they'll want to sleep with you. Or get this haircut because women will find you attractive and want to go home with you. Or buy this car to look powerful and impress women. Or just think about the business model of some of these sports bars. "We sell food. And also, there are a lot of half-naked women here!" We've grown accustomed to it, but when you think about it, it just doesn't make any sense.

Or think about how sex is portrayed in the media. How many movies' plots are completely centered around "trying to get laid"? Or how many television shows glorify the one night stand and trying to get with as many women as possible? Movies and TV portray guys going out to have sex with different women every night of the week. And guys who are not having sex regularly are mocked and ridiculed in media today.

This is an obsession! Society is completely and absolutely obsessed with sex. And it's incredibly unhealthy. We've been taught since we were very young that the only thing worth talking about or pursuing in the world is sex. And that's just not true. The reality is, many of the television and movie characters

THE MOST UNCOMFORTABLE CHAPTER EVER   63

that you see portrayed today would be diagnosed with a sex addiction. They're constantly thinking about, scheming about, and pursuing sexual conquests. And we've been told that this is normal. That this is what you, as a man, should be doing.

Guys. Let me clear something up for you. The way the media and society portray sexuality is not healthy. *You've been born into a society that has told you that having a sex addiction is part of being a man.* You've been told your whole life that sex is everything.

It's not. It's one thing.

And in the grand scheme of life, it's actually a pretty small part. Sex is a great thing in the right context. But it's not the purpose of life. It's not something to use to gauge your manliness. And it's not something to obsess over.

This is why you feel so trapped. We've taken sexuality to a level that it was never intended to go. Naturally, you would struggle with lust anyway. But being submerged in a culture that is constantly throwing sexually charged images and ideas in your face, telling you that you should be having more sex than is humanly possible, and that having a sex addiction is the norm, has created a whole new struggle that every man has to deal with today.

Seeing And Looking

So a big part of the reason that you struggle with lust and wanting sex is because you're seeing it everywhere you go. The movies you watch, the billboards you see, the radio you hear, your social media feed, even walking down the hallway at school is filled with sexuality. And every time you see something stimulating, it pushes your sex drive just a little bit higher. It seems unavoidable. And the reality is that it is unavoidable. At this point in the world we're simply not going to be able to go through our day without seeing something sexually charging. But there's a way around it.

Your eyes are always working. As long as they're open, you see things. You can't help that. So you can't help it when commercials start off with girls in bikinis holding beer. It just popped up, and you saw it. You can't help it when the girl in front of you in gym class starts stretching unexpectedly. You can't help when a new billboard is advertising more than just new low deals. You see things all the time, and you can't help it. You can't control what you see, but you can control what you look at.

What's the difference? I'm glad you asked. Seeing happens all the time. It's just what your eyes do. Looking is intentional. Looking is on purpose. Looking is seeing that a commercial started with a girl in a bikini and watching the whole thing. Looking is noticing that the girl is stretching in front of you and moving to another machine to get a better view. Looking is driving past a billboard and not watching where you're going, and instead checking out these great deals. Looking is intentional.

So the new rule is, *you can see, but you can't look.*

You can see. But you can't look. So when you see a woman jogging, you know to look somewhere else. When you see a movie scene that you shouldn't be watching, you stare at the floor until it's over. When a group of attractive women walks by on the beach, you don't watch them leave. You look away.

You can see. But you can't look. Got it? Awesome. You'll start to see a big difference in your life as soon as you put this into practice. It will make you feel better about how you think about women and will help you get that sex drive of yours under control.

Taking The Edge Off

I'd like to transition our conversation about sex and make it even more uncomfortable for you. Let's talk about masturbation. Yay! Yeah, I know. It's not something you want to talk about, or ever talk about, or even think about really. I get it. But it's important that we talk about this because there are a lot of mixed messages going around about this topic, and I want us to get a few things straight.

You may have heard the catch phrase, "Sex can wait, Masturbate!" at some point in your life. I think the person or people that came up with it had good intentions, but weren't really thinking from a Christian perspective. The Bible doesn't address this topic directly. So everyone is kind of entitled to their opinion, but I'm going to argue to you that while masturbation itself may not be biblically forbidden, it still has no place in the life of a man of God. Check out this verse from Mathew. This is Jesus talking:

> *You have heard the commandment that says, 'You must not commit adultery.' But I say, anyone who even looks at a woman with lust has already committed adultery with her in his heart. 28-29*

"Whoa. Wait a minute. What's Jesus talking about here? Have I committed adultery like... a thousand times?" No. That's not what He means. To me this verse basically means, no, you shouldn't be having sex outside of marriage, but you also shouldn't be thinking about doing it either. Ever.

So let's get real for a moment. What kind of thoughts are you having during masturbation? Are they pure? Do they involve lust of any kind? If we're being honest, we know masturbation is a problem. And I don't believe that one can be participating in this activity and having pure thoughts. It just needs to be eliminated. And eliminating it will become much easier when you've also eliminated the visual stimulation you shouldn't be looking at.

The Real Deal

So. We've talked about your sex drive. We've talked about managing it. We've talked about masturbation... I feel like I'm forgetting something... right. Sex. Let's talk about sex. I'll just get right to the point. Sex needs to wait. You need to wait until you're married to have sex. To start with, I think there's a pretty strong biblical argument for this.

Paul talks about it in I Corinthians 7.

The Old Testament laws speak about it all the time. Exodus 22 is a pretty good example.

And Genesis 2 pretty much starts the whole Bible by describing what marriage and sex are supposed to look like.

There are a lot of verses that talk about this, and I'd encourage you to Google them for yourself. Do your own research. Remember, a man of God knows what he believes. But you've probably heard a lot of these reasons before. So here's one more.

A lot of guys often ask the question, "Well, how far can I go?" I like to answer this question with another question. *Is she your wife?* Because if she's not, you don't get to do anything.

Until you are married; she is not yours. Until you're married, you don't know how long you're going to be with this girl. What if you break up? What if she gets married to another guy years from now? That's another man's wife you slept with. Until you're married, she is not yours. Until you're married, she's potentially someone else's. It doesn't matter if you're in love. It doesn't matter if you "know she's the one." She and her husband get to enjoy having sex. You and your wife get to enjoy having sex. That's it.

How dare you take that gift from another man? How dare you take that from her? Sex before marriage is irresponsible. But it's also selfish. A real man of God recognizes that he lives in a sex-obsessed culture and doesn't buy into it. A real man knows that he wants sex, but understands that he needs to wait. And does it. It's not easy. But it needs to be done. So he does it. That's the behavior of a man of God.

Until she's yours, she's another man's wife. I know you don't want someone sleeping with your future wife. Stay away from his.

Wrapping It Up

That got kind of heavy. But I think it's important that we take this seriously. We live in a world that has glorified and allows sex in any capacity. And you need to be the example that leads the way against this mentality. Recognize that you are set up for failure, and then succeed anyway. Realize that the world is telling you nothing but lies about sex, and find the truth for yourself. Know that this is going to be a battle for you for a long time, especially if college is in your future. Make a decision today to represent God as a man in this capacity. I know you're up to it.

Check out these action steps, and let's keep moving.

Action Steps

Do you agree that our society is obsessed with sex? Why? What are some examples?

_____

_____

_____

_____

What are some things you need to stop looking at?

_____

_____

_____

_____

In your own words, why does sex need to wait until marriage?

_____

_____

_____

_____

Write out a commitment to not have sex until you're married. Then sign it. This is just between you and God. So take it seriously.

_____

_____

_____

_____

Name _____ Signature _____

LET'S TALK ABOUT PORN

Just Another Day

I remember the exact day it happened. It was kind of a gloomy fall day. I was about eleven. I was outside with my friends playing football because that's what we did every day. But at the end of our game, some of the guys started talking about this website they had found, and how I *just had to* check it out. So I waited for an opportunity, logged in, and clicked.

The screen that opened up was unlike anything I had ever seen before. I didn't know what to do, so I panicked. I turned the computer off. I didn't close the window, I just hit the power button, and quite literally ran away. But that was all it took. I had encountered pornography for the first time. I didn't know the decision I was making. I didn't know that I had started a struggle I would deal with for years after. I had no idea. Maybe you can relate to this story. Most guys your age can.

9 out of 10 guys are exposed to internet porn before the age of 18.

7 out of 10 guys your age admit to hiding their internet activity from their parents.

I hope you didn't think it was just you. It's not. And because of how prevalent it's become in the world, we need to have a conversation about something that nobody wants to talk about. You guessed it. We need to talk about porn.

What You Don't Know

Here's the thing. You probably already know that porn is bad. You've been told that it's bad by your church, parents, teachers, whoever. And if we're being honest, you probably just instinctively know that it's not good. There are safe-search filters that keep it away; there are screens that pop up that make you verify that you are in fact trying to watch pornography, there are articles and blogs that talk about it being bad, celebrities are talking about their struggles with it… you probably intellectually understand that it's not good. But that's not the same as understanding *why* it's a problem. So here are some things I wish someone had told me when I was in high school about porn.

Porn Is Addictive

You might not know this about porn, but it has a highly addictive nature. Porn addiction functions much the same as any other drug addiction functions in the brain. The really simplified version is that when your brain sees something it likes it releases this chemical called dopamine. When this chemical is released, we experience pleasure. All kinds of things cause dopamine to be released like exercise, hitting a home run, a good phone conversation, and of course, sex. The problem is, porn causes a huge release of dopamine in the brain. Basically, this is a high. And your brain wants to get the release of dopamine again, and it remembers how. It remembers where you were, how you got it, what the weather

was like, the temperature of the room, what you were smell-
ing... everything. So your body develops this desire to see
porn again, to get that release of dopamine. Obviously, it's
more complicated than that, but it helps to have at least some
understanding of how something like porn can be, and is,
addictive.

Some people have even gone so far as to say that porn is more
addictive than physical drugs because porn never leaves the
body. Eventually, marijuana, cocaine, heroin, physical drugs,
work their way out of your system, and this can make it easier
to break a habit. But pornography lives in your memory. It
never leaves once you've seen it. And this makes it incredibly
difficult to break a pornography addiction once one has started.

In addition to that, much like in other drug use, your brains
starts to gain a resilience to pornography. The more porn you
see the more your brain gets used to it, and you start to get less
of a high. Kind of how drug addicts progress from a seemingly
harmless "gateway drug" into more and more hardcore drug
use, pornography addicts find themselves seeking more and
more aggressive forms of pornography. So what may start out
as "harmless" softcore pornography, can easily progress into
hardcore, bondage, rape, and even child pornography. It's a
dangerous slippery slope that can lead to broken relationships,
lost opportunities, and even jail time.

I don't have any stats or research to prove this theory, but I
believe a high percentage of men that look at pornography
have no idea they're addicted. But they are. The problem with
addiction is you only realize you're addicted when you try to
stop. And then it's too late. If you think it won't happen to
you, you are incredibly naïve. Save yourself the struggle and
just stay away from porn altogether.

Porn Alters Your Thoughts

I recently watched the movie *Creed*. It's a movie about a young man with a dream of being a boxer who enlists legendary boxer, Rocky Balboa, to help him train. I really enjoyed the film, but something interesting happened to me the next day. I found myself shadowboxing around the house.

I found myself imagining myself in the ring floating like a butterfly and stinging like a bee. I was ducking imaginary hooks, deflecting invisible jabs, and delivering fictitious knockout blows all throughout the next day. But here's the thing. I've never boxed in my life! I've never worn boxing gloves, hit a heavy bag, or learned how to throw a proper punch. But here I was throwing punches and dancing around my living room boxing ring.

Here's the point. That movie altered my thoughts. I don't box, but I couldn't stop thinking about it. And that was just one movie. How much more would watching pornography on a regular basis alter the way you think throughout your day? Pretty soon, you'll start looking at women as objects to have sex with. Pretty soon, you'll start thinking that violent and demeaning sex is normal. Pretty soon, you'll start to think that the only reason to have a relationship is to get laid. Pretty soon you'll start talking to women like they do in the videos, and start getting other ideas from them.

If you think porn isn't affecting the way you think, you're a bit delusional. You're only fooling yourself, and you're playing a very dangerous game. Pornography will not stop infiltrating your mind until it has you. Until it consumes every thought and idea you have. It will dig into your subconscious until it has changed who you are into a womanizer, pervert, and sex addict. Pornography wants to control you and change you, and it has no place in the mind of a man of God.

Pornography Is Fake

I like *Harry Potter*. The books, the movies, I think it's a really fun story. Maybe you like *Harry Potter* as well, or maybe you like it but won't admit it. That's fine. Now I want you to imagine watching one of the *Harry Potter* movies with your friends. You all sit down, make some popcorn, make jokes throughout; it's a fun time. But then after the movie, one of your friends stands up and says, "Where can I buy a magic wand like Harry Potter's?"

In all seriousness. What would you think? That would be odd right? You'd probably make fun of him, or maybe just not know how to respond. Because everyone that watches *Harry Potter* has a clear understanding that what's happening in the movie isn't real. It in no way represents reality.

Porn is the same way. It in no way represents reality. Absolutely nothing about porn is real. But for some reason guys seem to be having a hard time separating what they see in pornography from the real world. Guys today are watching a directed production on a screen, and believing that it represents sex correctly. And nothing could be further from the truth. The real problem here is that many guys your age are learning about sex from pornography.

You need to understand that pornography is scripted, unrealistic, and imaginative. Pornography is nothing more than actors on a screen fulfilling outrageous fantasies and is no more realistic than any action hero movie you've seen. It's all made up. It's all fake. And it's teaching guys your age a super unhealthy view of sexuality.

Pornography promotes a sexuality where the man is king, and the woman is there only for his pleasure. Violence is encouraged through, hitting, restraining, and choking. Women are expected to be perfectly manicured, made up, willing and submissive. The man dominates the bedroom taking what he wants and forcing the woman to do degrading acts. This is not a healthy view of sexuality. And it certainly does not model how a man of God treats his wife in the bedroom. You need to understand that what porn is promoting is not healthy. And it's not what sex will, or should, look like.

Learning about sex from porn is like learning to do a magic trick by watching *Harry Potter*. Much like the *Harry Potter* movies calls what they do *magic*, pornography calls what they do *sex*. And it's not. If you're learning about sex from pornography you need to unlearn what you think is true. Pornography is fake, and it promotes a very unhealthy sexuality.

There are so many more reasons to avoid pornography like the abusive way pornography actresses are treated, or the reality that those are your sisters in Christ on screen, or the damage the porn industry is causing to society in general, or simply the amount of time it wastes. I could write an entire book just on why pornography is a problem. But I'll stop here, and hope I've made my point. *It's dangerous.* And it needs to be avoided.

"What Should I Do If..."

So, I'm going to go out on a limb here and assume you've seen pornography. Maybe it was on purpose, maybe it was an accident, maybe it was a while ago, or maybe you're currently addicted, and nobody knows about it. The thing about pornography addiction is that it's a huge issue. So trying to do justice to it in just one chapter really isn't enough. I'm going to share some of the best tips I know of to get you started. But this book isn't designed to help you quit pornography. If you only take one thing from this chapter, let be that pornography is dangerous, and you need to run away from it. If you're struggling with a pornography addiction, don't wait. Don't even hesitate. You need to start taking action against it immediately.

Tell Someone

Far and away, the most helpful thing to do when trying to stop looking at pornography is to tell someone about your struggle. It's also perhaps the scariest thing to do. But nothing is going to help you find success faster than enlisting help. I know that there's someone in your life that wants to help you get out of this. Maybe your parents, or youth pastor, neighbor, teacher, friend's dad, whoever it might be.

As men, we often want to do things ourselves. We don't want help. We want to win the battle and have ourselves to thank for our success. We want to kick down the door and kill the dragon with a sword. We don't like help. Please don't let pride get in the way of your success. Pornography is too dangerous and destructive to allow in your life. Even if you were able to beat porn alone, why would you? Why not get away from it faster? Why not let other men of God into your life and help you out of this struggle?

You need to enlist help. And this doesn't have to be weird. I'm not asking you to find someone to lay hands on you or to start some deep psychotherapy sessions or anything like that. Getting help can look a lot like getting coffee with another guy and just talking about your struggle. Being real and honest, but doing so in a way we understand. Maybe you guys should meet for wings or pizza. Maybe talking while you shoot pool or play ping pong. Be creative. But don't wait. Identify who you think you could talk to quickly, and tell them. Just get it over with. You'll be glad you did.

Identify Your Triggers

You need to start to figure out where, when, and why you look at porn. These are called triggers. Things that make you want to look at pornography. Things like seeing a racy scene in a movie, or seeing a woman jogging, being home alone, or feeling overly stressed. All of these things can make you feel like you want to look at porn. Essentially, they trigger you.

A good second step is finding your triggers. What's going on when you want to look at porn? Where are you? Who else is there? What are you doing? What are you feeling? Start to write down and keep track of when you feel triggered to look at porn. And when you start to see patterns, make changes. Once you identify what your triggers are, you need to start avoiding or eliminating them. So maybe you find that when you're home alone, you want to look at porn. If that's the case, you need to change something. Maybe you need to not be home alone, so you go to a friend's house for an hour or so. Maybe you need to tell someone you're going to be home alone, and don't want to look at porn. Or maybe you can get an app that doesn't allow you internet access for the time you're home alone. Be creative, but when you recognize a trigger, you need to make a change.

Maybe you need to stop staying up so late. Maybe you need to stop hanging out with guys that talk about porn. Maybe you need to stop staring at girls at the gym. Maybe you need to turn the WiFi off of your phone. Whatever you need to do, do it. You need to make eliminating porn a priority in your life, and that will require sacrifice. But you need to know, that it will absolutely be worth it. Recognize why you look at porn, and make changes.

Check Out Some Better Resources

Like I said, porn is a pretty huge topic. And I'm not going to try to tell you how to fix an addiction in one chapter. It's going to take a lot of work. It's going to hurt. And it might take longer than you think. But you have to get started. Pornography has absolutely no place in the life of a man of God. I'm going to give you two other books that you can check out if you're trapped in a porn addiction. They are:

Every Young Man's Battle
by Fred Stoker and Stephen Arterburn
and
Pure Eyes
by Craig Gross

Both of these books are excellent resources that I've read personally. I know that they will give you more resources, and empower you to make the change in your life that you want to see. They're both focused on learning what it means to have a healthy view of sexuality as a man of God. If you need more help than this book gives you, I hope you'll check them out.

Finding Freedom

I want you to find freedom from pornography. This is one of those areas where creating good habits early in life will drastically impact the rest of your life. Pornography will impact your friendships, your dating life, your work life, your sleep, and your marriage if not eliminated completely. Don't take the risk. Start making good habits now.

If you've never looked at porn, I cannot stress to you how fortunate you are. Stay away from it. I genuinely and truly believe that pornography is the vilest and most disgusting substance on the planet. Pornography is the lowest humans have fallen, and we have to work together to eliminate it. If you've avoided it this long, congratulations. Don't throw it away.

If you're looking at porn currently, please don't wait. Please don't waste time trying to get it done on your own. Please get help. And please get started right away. It may seem harmless. It may seem like you could quit any time you want to. These are lies created by our enemy. You need to run away from it. You need to eradicate it from your life.

I hope you will get away, and stay away from pornography. It really is a problem. And it really is dangerous. Check out the action steps for this chapter, and let's keep rolling.

Action Steps

Why is pornography so dangerous? Can you think of some other reasons that aren't listed in this chapter?

_____

_____

_____

_____

Who is someone you could talk to about pornography?

_____

_____

When are you going to talk to them?

_____

_____

Start making a list of triggers in your life.

_____

_____

_____

Write out a prayer to God asking Him to give you the strength to make the changes you need to make

_____

_____

_____

_____

Commit this verse to memory: 1 Corinthians 6:18

> *Run from sexual sin! No other sin so clearly*
> *affects the body as this one does.*
> *For sexual immorality is a sin against your own body.*

DIARY OF AN AVERAGE GUY

Boys Will Be Boys

So there's this crazy thing happening in high schools everywhere, and somehow it's being overlooked. Bullying. Now, I know what you're thinking. You're probably sick of hearing about bullying. Bullying seems to be the new buzzword people are throwing around to talk about kids being mean to each other. But unfortunately, it has become much more than that.

When I talk about bullying, I'm not talking about what you and your friends do to each other to pick on each other. Things like shoulder punching, the occasional pantsing, creating inappropriate nicknames for each other, and general prank-playing. These things have their place in the male society and can even contribute to bonding if done in a kind way. But bullying is another level of this. Bullying is done with the intention of harming someone emotionally, physically, or socially.

Bullying causes others to be afraid, feel alone, and dread social interactions. Not the behavior of friends. The truth is, bullying can have lasting effects on a person, particularly since much of it is done during developmental years of one's life. Students are being physically harmed, socially humiliated, and emotionally tormented in your school. And guess what? As a man of God, you need to do something about it.

But First, A Bible Story

Before we go on, I want us to take a look at a story in the Bible. In Mathew 25, Jesus tells an interesting story that I think applies to this situation very well. He tells us about what it's going to look like after we die. Creepy right? So this is Jesus talking, and verses 34-40 read like this:

> "Then the King will say to those on his right, 'Come, you who are blessed by my Father, inherit the Kingdom prepared for you from the creation of the world. For I was hungry, and you fed me. I was thirsty, and you gave me a drink. I was a stranger, and you invited me into your home. I was naked, and you gave me clothing. I was sick, and you cared for me. I was in prison, and you visited me.'

> "Then these righteous ones will reply, 'Lord, when did we ever see you hungry and feed you? Or thirsty and give you something to drink? Or a stranger and show you hospitality? Or naked and give you clothing? When did we ever see you sick or in prison and visit you?'

> "And the King will say, 'I tell you the truth, when you did it to *one of the least of these* my brothers and sisters, you were doing it to me!' (Emphasis added)

Maybe you've heard this before, maybe you haven't, but here's the thing; I think we tend to take this verse a little too literally. We start thinking like, "Well, if I ever see a hungry person, I'll feed them I guess. And if I see a naked guy, I'm probably just going to run away, and you're not supposed to let strangers into your house…" Yeah, I get it. That's probably good thinking actually. But that's not the point of these verses.

The point of these verses is to draw attention to a certain group of people. Jesus mentions the "Least of These" in this section. That's kind of a weird phrase, isn't it? It's not really one we use today. So let's look at how Jesus used the phrase to see if we can figure out what it might mean, and then what it means for us today.

Why Wouldn't You Wear Pants If You Could..?

So let's look at who Jesus references specifically when he mentions the least of these. He talks about:

The hungry
The thirsty
Strangers
The naked
The sick
And the imprisoned

The thing that all of these situations have in common is they're all helpless situations. The people in these situations can't do anything about it. Think about it. If any of these people could do something about their situation, they would. Right?

Nobody would be hungry if they had access to food. They would eat! Nobody just has bottles of water laying around and is dying of thirst. Nobody would be friendless if they knew a solution. Nobody owns clothes but refuses to wear them (well I guess some people do. But let's disregard that for now). Many prisoners want visitors, but not all get them. These situations require outside help. Jesus is describing people that are in need of help, but can't help themselves. That's what Jesus meant by the least of these, and that's how we're going to define "the least of these" from here on out. *People who are in need of help, but can't help themselves.*

I've said it before, but I will reemphasize, you are not going to be a man of God. You *are* a man of God. Right now. And you have responsibilities that come with being that. And one of them, a really big one, is "the least of these" in your life. There are going to be a lot of people, especially in high school, that need your help, but can't help themselves —which brings us back to bullying.

As a man of God, you can't let it happen. If you see someone getting bullied, or hear about it, or know about it, or hear a rumor that someone is getting bullied, you have an obligation to do something about it. It's your job as a man of God to stand up for the oppressed. It's your role to be a protector for those who can't protect themselves. You're a man. And you have to defend those that God has entrusted to you.

But What About...

Now, I know what you're thinking. "Some people are in need of help, but just *won't* help themselves." Or, "Some people need help, but they don't want my help." Or maybe even, "Some people need my help, but they don't deserve it." Yeah, these can be tough situations. But when we run into something like this, we have to remember to think big picture. We have to remember our goal.

So when someone won't help themselves, how do we show them Christ's love? We help them help themselves. When someone doesn't want our help, how do we show them Christ's love? We pray for them, and we help them anyway. And when someone doesn't deserve our help? We recognize that Christ forgave us, we have to forgive, and we help them out anyway. These people are still the least of these. They still need help. And they still deserve your help.

The NABV (New Andy Buckwalter Version)

So you remember that story Jesus told in Mathew? (It was like two pages ago) I'm going to reword it into a way that might make it a little more practical for someone your age. After all, you don't own a house, you probably don't know many inmates, and I'm sure your school has a dress code that prohibits nudity. Here's how it might read if Jesus was in high school.

> "Then the King will say to those on his right, 'Brah! Thank you so much! Some jerks stole my lunch money, and you spotted me. Someone started a rumor about me, and you stopped it. A bully made a joke about me, and you didn't laugh. This big guy was shoving me, and you stepped in. I was being bullied, and you defended me. I was being laughed at, and you stood up for me. I was alone, and you befriended me.'"

These people are the least of these in your life. Jesus talks about the hungry, the poor, the clothes-less. You probably won't see much of that in your high school. High school wasn't exactly Jesus' target audience at the time. But you will see bullies in high school. And you will see the bullied in high school.

Let me make something very clear to you. You have an obligation to these people. It is your job to make sure people in your circle of influence are not being bullied. It's your responsibility to make sure that everyone you know feels safe going to school, getting on the bus, going home, eating lunch.

And if you see bullying, and refuse to do something about it, you're not fulfilling your role as a man of God. I don't know if you're afraid of what people will think, or if you're worried about getting bullied yourself, or if you just genuinely don't care about these other people. But if you're claiming to be a man of God, and you're not doing anything to defend the least of these in your life, you're not upholding your end of the deal. You're not fulfilling your responsibilities, and you need to seriously examine why.

You Know What To Do

I know it's easier said than done. I know it's easier to just laugh along and say something like,

"He doesn't mind"

"He's used to it"

"He brings it on himself"

"This will help him stop being so annoying"

"It'll build character..."

Every one of those excuses is exactly that. Excuses. Men of God don't make excuses. They produce change. They conquer problems. They see someone in need, and they charge headfirst into the battle. (The metaphorical battle. I'm not suggesting you fight someone). They're the first ones to stand up for someone.

You know what you should do. You know bullying when you see it. People are going to say mean things. I get that. Guys are going to shout and push and get angry from time to time. I get that. I'm not talking about that. I'm talking about the guy who's afraid to change in the locker room because someone is going to ridicule him. I'm talking about the guy who hates walking down the hallway because of the names they call him. The guy who isn't allowed to be himself because of the rumors and punching.

You know it when you see it. You know when it's out of hand. You know when you should intervene. And when you know you should do something; you have to do it. Check out what James says in chapter 4:

Remember, it is a sin to know what you ought to do and then not do it.

That's a good one to commit to memory. It's James 4:17, and it's one of the mottos of a man of God. When a man of God knows what he should do, he takes action. Sitting back and doing nothing is no longer an option.

Average Archibald

Here's what I want you to take away from this. The odds are pretty good that if you're reading this, you're just kind of one of the guys. You might be popular, or you might have a small group of close friends. You might not be very tall, but you're probably not super short. You're probably not being bullied, and you're probably not bullying anyone. This is probably the case for you and most of your friends.

High school for you is neither stimulating nor boring. You feel safe when you go to school. You wake up and feel completely neutral about going to school. You're not dreading it, but you're not necessarily excited about it either.

Everyone deserves that. Everyone deserves at least that.

It's not much. But everyone deserves to wake up in the morning and go to school feeling safe. Feeling confident that when they enter the school, they're not going to be harassed. They're not going to be made fun of, and they're not going to be touched. They deserve that. And you and your friends cannot sit by and just "Let things happen." **You** need to be the one that initiates change. **You** need to be the first one to stand up for the least of these. Because if there's one thing a man of God doesn't care about, it's committing social suicide. Even if people laugh at you, and they might. Even if people don't support you, and they might not. You know what's right. And you need to do it. You need to recognize the least of these in your life. And a big part of that are students that are being bullied.

It's going to take courage. But I know you're up for it. Maybe you need to talk to a teacher about a problem you've seen. Maybe you just need to invite someone to sit at your table. Maybe you need to talk to a bully directly. Be looking for the least of these in your life. Who can you help that needs help?

Check out these action steps, and let's move into our last chapter. (How sad!)

Action Steps

How would you define the Least of These?

_____

_____

_____

_____

What could be some consequences of standing up for the least of these in your life?

_____

_____

_____

_____

Other than people being bullied, who else might be the least of these in your life? Who else needs help but can't help themselves?

_____

_____

_____

_____

Who is someone you need to stand up for?

_____

_____

_____

_____

TO FORGIVE,
OR NOT TO FORGIVE...

Holding on to anger is like drinking poison,
and expecting the other person to die

Aim Small, Miss Small

One of my favorite movies of all time is *The Patriot* starring Mel Gibson. It's a movie about a guy named Benjamin Martin and takes place during the American Revolutionary War. Throughout this movie, Mel Gibson's character loses his home. He loses some of his children. And, at some points, pretty much loses his mind. It's a great story about overcoming adversity, fighting for what's right, and of course, revenge.

One scene that stands out to me in the movie occurs just after Benjamin Martin loses his home. A group of British soldiers rides in, takes what they want, and then burns his house to the ground. And then, just to be a total jerk, one of the officers shoots one of his kids. Right in front of him. Needless to say, he's not pleased. So he runs into his burning house, grabs all of the weapons and guns he can hold, brings two of his living sons with him, and hunts down this group of soldiers.

He and his sons hide in the woods, wait for the soldiers to ride by, and then shoot them all down. The scene ends with the main character going absolutely insane on these soldiers with a tomahawk. It's pretty violent. But every man in the audience can relate to the desire for vengeance. And this guy gets it. That's what makes the scene so powerful.

See, as men, we're naturally programmed to want to save the day. We naturally want to take things into our own hands and set things straight. When a wrong is committed, we want to right it. When someone hurts us, we want to hurt them back. And in some cases, when someone is hurt badly or killed, we want to kill them back. But is this the model that Christ demonstrated for us? (I'll give you a hint. No.)

Talking About Forgiveness

I want to talk about forgiveness in this chapter. Forgiveness isn't something we really talk about as men very often, but it's important. I probably wouldn't have seen *The Patriot* more than once if that scene had ended with Benjamin Martin sitting down with the British soldiers and forgiving them. It's just not something we crave. But it is one of those things that you need to start practicing now because it doesn't get easier as you go. But before you can start practicing forgiveness, we should probably take a look at what it is.

Forgiveness is a pretty simple concept in theory. I mean, we teach it to children. Remember when you were in elementary school and someone did something that bothered you? At the time, it was probably something like taking the crayon you wanted or cutting in line, but regardless of why you were upset, you were taught how to handle the situation.

The teacher would sit you and little Johnny down, and talk to him first.

"Johnny, did you take a crayon from Carl Jr?"

And Johnny would respond, "Yes, Misses Appleglasses."

And then she would respond with every adult's favorite phrase ever; "What do you say?"

And Johnny would know he's supposed to say, "I'm sorry," which is basically the kid version of asking for forgiveness. We don't really explain it to children that way, but that's what's happening. We're teaching children that you should apologize, and ask for forgiveness from the person you've wronged. That's the first half of the conversation. Then Miss Appleglasses turned to you.

"Now Carl Jr. What do you say to Johnny?"

To which, you should respond with something along the lines of "It's okay." Which, again, is kind of like the kid version of "I forgive you." You've done something wrong to me, but you've admitted it, so I forgive you for doing the thing that was wrong. Pretty simple concept really. But we all know it isn't that easy. And it definitely doesn't get easier.

The Time Out Corner

Let's expand on our classroom analogy a little further. What usually happened next? Did you and little Johnny Appleseed just go back to playing? Probably not. What probably happened next was you went back to the LEGO table, but Johnny was still in trouble. He probably got a warning or had to go play somewhere else, or in the most extreme of situations, he would have to go into a time out.

Do you remember time out? Time out was the worst! "Go sit over there and watch other people have fun." It was brutal. In my elementary school, we used to have to go to "The Wall"—which was exactly what it sounded like. It was the outside of the building by the playground, and if you were in trouble, you had to go stand on the wall. It was on the top of a hill, there was no shade, and there were often bees! It was brutal. Everyone could see that you were in trouble, you were hot, and your friends were still playing without you.

But wait a minute. Why is little Johnny on the wall? Didn't he apologize? Didn't you forgive him? Yes. But he's still in trouble. And he should be.

Justice Beaver

There's an important distinction that we need to make here between justice, revenge, and forgiveness. Forgiveness isn't justice, and it isn't revenge. I think the three have kind of blended together, because they often take place at the same time.

Justice and revenge have to do with what happens to the person who did the offense. Justice describes when the person gets what they should get. For example, if someone steals twenty dollars, they have to give it back. If someone cheats on a test, they lose some points. And if someone takes the center chip on a plate of nachos (the nucleus) before the proper time, they can't watch the game with you anymore. Maybe not the last one, but you get the point. *Justice means a fair response to the injustice.*

Revenge is quite different. Revenge is you getting what *you* want. So if someone lifts your wallet, you want to punch them in the face. When someone cheats in football, you want to deliver a late hit. And when someone takes the center nacho, you want to smash the whole plate in his face. Enough about nachos. Revenge isn't justice. Revenge is not trying to make something right; *revenge is trying to hurt someone for what they did.* Revenge doesn't help; it makes it worse.

But the interesting thing is, you can have justice, or revenge, or both, but still not forgiveness. And you can have forgiveness without revenge or justice. Because forgiveness is not about what happens to the other person. *Forgiveness has to do with what happens within you.* Forgiveness is you deciding not to be angry about it, and not to be angry at them. And that's the hard part.

I think it's hard because we misunderstand what forgiveness is, and who benefits from it. We often confuse forgiveness with the absence of justice. But that's not true. Remember what happened in elementary school? You can forgive your friends, but they still have to go to time out. Forgiving someone doesn't mean there are no consequences for their actions.

Similarly, we often think that forgiveness means things go back to normal. That we have to be best friends who have secret handshakes and play tennis together. But that's not the case either. Forgiving someone doesn't mean we have to be friends. Forgiving someone doesn't mean we have to spend time with them. It doesn't mean we have to trust them. It doesn't even mean we have to like them. It just means we forgive them. It just means letting go of the negative feelings we have towards them. Forgiving someone has nothing to do with what happens to that person. Just how you decide to feel towards them.

So What's The Point?

So it's not revenge. And it's not justice... What's the point? Why take a whole chapter just to talk about forgiveness? Because it's important. For a lot of reasons, but one in particular. You ready for it? Here it is. *Forgiveness is freedom.* I started this chapter with a quote.

> *"Holding on to anger is like drinking poison,*
> *and expecting the other person to die."*

It's often attributed to Buddha, but nobody's really sure who said this. The point is pretty clear though, isn't it? When we refuse to forgive, we damage ourselves. We hurt ourselves. When you're holding on to anger, you can't be all you could be. You can't enjoy things the way you could. You can't focus on things you need to. And most importantly, you can't love the way you're supposed to.

The crazy thing is, we think denying someone forgiveness is accomplishing something. There's a part of us that feels like if we can just stay angry long enough, something will happen. Doesn't it? If you continue to hold this grudge, then the person you're mad at will somehow know it and be able to feel your anger. You'll be able to keep them up at night, prevent them from enjoying life, and leave them with a sense of guilt in everything they do. But it's just not true. Much like forgiving only helps you, holding on to a grudge only hurts you. Nobody else.

When you refuse to forgive someone, you give them power over you. And I know you don't like to do that. But it's the truth. Forgiveness gives you freedom from that. Forgiveness gives you your power back. It's important. But don't just take my word for it. We have a model to follow. Let's see what the man himself has to say.

I Think I Would Have Just Killed Them All

Jesus actually talks quite a lot about forgiveness, probably because it's such a difficult topic. But it's one thing to talk about it, and another thing to live it out. And this is Jesus we're talking about, so you can be sure he also lived it out. I want us to take a look at, what I think is, one of the most overlooked verses in the Bible.

When they came to a place called The Skull they nailed him to the cross...Jesus said, "Father, forgive them, for they don't know what they are doing." –Luke 23:33-34

Let's look at the situation surrounding this verse. The night starts off with one of Jesus' best bros completely stabbing him in the back. Judas betrays Jesus to the Pharisees and officials. For money. Then Jesus gets arrested —which is frustrating all by itself. Especially considering He hadn't done anything wrong. Then His other friends bail on Him. All the other disciples run away because they don't want to be guilty by association. Then He stands through a series of fake trials, where people say terrible lies about Him all night. And He eventually finds Himself in front of Pilate. Finally. A rational person who knows right from wrong, and whose job it is to do the right thing. He'll help.

False. Pilate finds nothing wrong with Him. But, instead of doing his job, he decides to just let an angry mob decide what's going to happen to Jesus. They drag Jesus outside and beat the crud out of Him. People punch Him in the face. They pull His beard out. They spit on Him. They *spit* on Him... that's disgusting. They jam a crown of thorns into His head. They scourge Him, which is like whipping someone until their skin falls off. They make Him carry His cross until He collapses. Then they drag Him to the top of a hill, nail Him to a cross. I'll repeat that, *nail*, like with a hammer, Him to a cross, and stand it up. Then they point and laugh. He's exhausted. He's in a lot of pain. He's humiliated. He's been disrespected. And He's dying.

And at this point. Jesus has a decision to make.

I don't know about you, but I'd be thinking a lot more like Benjamin Martin with his tomahawk, and a lot less about forgiveness. But that's not what the verse says happens. Jesus, having been treated like less than an animal, looks down at the very people who are torturing Him to death... and forgives them. Not revenge. Not even justice. He just forgives them.

Now that. Is manly.

I know forgiveness can seem hard. I know that forgiveness doesn't come naturally. I know it's not always what we want. But look at the example we've been given. One of the last things Jesus did before He died was to forgive. If we're modeling our life after His, you better know that forgiveness is going to play a major role in it.

I Know It's Hard

I know. It's not that easy. I know you're not Jesus. I know that the person you're not forgiving really did hurt you. Maybe it was an old friend who started a rumor about you. Maybe it's a teammate who cheated and got the starting position. Maybe someone stole something from you. Maybe it was a girl who lied to you. Maybe it was your dad, and you haven't forgiven him for walking out. Or maybe it was you. And you just won't let yourself off the hook.

Forgiveness gets really difficult when we separate it from revenge and justice because we start to realize that sometimes we're going to have to forgive someone when there wasn't justice. And there wasn't revenge. Sometimes, we're going to have to forgive first.

I know it's hard. I know you're angry for good reason. And it might take a while before you're really ready to honestly say that you're not anymore. You might even need some help in dealing with how you feel. Maybe you need to talk to a friend about it. Maybe your parents, youth pastor, or uncle can help. And in some cases, you might even need to get some counseling to help you let go. I know it can be hard. I told you it takes practice.

But knowing the value of forgiveness at your age is going to help. Recognizing that you only hurt yourself by harboring anger and give power to other people over you by holding a grudge should help you recognize that you need to start working on forgiveness now. Jesus modeled it for you. And you need to start practicing it today.

One last time, check out these action steps and keep rolling.

Action Steps

Why is forgiveness so hard?

_____

_____

_____

_____

What is the difference between forgiveness, justice, and revenge in your own words?

_____

_____

_____

_____

Why is forgiveness so important?

_____

_____

_____

_____

Who could you talk to, to help you work through forgiving someone?

_____

_____

_____

_____

Who do you need to forgive today?

_____

_____

_____

_____

THE LAST CHAPTER

You did it! You read the whole book! I knew you could do it. It's been quite the journey, hasn't it? I hope you enjoyed this book, and that you'll put some things you read and learned into practice. Let's recap some of the things we talked about. (Because I know it took some of you like six months to finish this book, and you've already forgotten).

We started off by redefining what it means to be a man in God's eyes. We talked about thinking big picture, and our goal being to hear, "Well done good and faithful servant." We talked about how society's definition of what it means to be a man is way off from what God thinks it means to be a man. And we wrote our own definition of what it means to be a man.

Then we talked about what you believe, and why you believe it. I encouraged you to wrestle with what you believe and to ask why. Why do you believe what you believe? Nobody ever asked me that, so I'm asking you. A real man knows what he believes, and why. Don't be afraid to ask the tough questions.

Focus time was next. We talked about finding a quiet time and place to spend time with God every day. We talked about why it's important, and some of the struggles that come along with it. Focus time is the ten minutes in the locker room before the big game. You sit in silence and refocus on your goal. Same with your focus time with God. You're focusing on your goal, and coming out ready to go.

Your price tag. Next, we talked about value. We talked about the importance of separating accomplishments from value. We talked about the price that God paid for you. We talked about the struggle of not feeling like enough. God loves you. He paid a high price for you. Don't ever question your value to Him again.

Then we got practical. We started talking about dating and girls. What you'd all been waiting for. We talked about what it meant to SCORE in a relationship, and how your relationships need to look differently from the world's. Your relationships are one way you represent Christ to the world. It's a way people see something different about you. But most importantly, we talked about how each and every girl you meet is a child of God. Your sister in Christ. And how she deserves a man of God in her relationships.

After dating, we talked about sex. This one got pretty real. We talked about some reasons sex needs to wait. We talked about how society is obsessed with sex, and how you need to not be. We talked about seeing and looking, and we talked about masturbation. This is a tough one, and you might need to reread it a few times. But a man of God respects sex for what it was meant to be, and is willing to wait.

And then there was porn. Just in case you weren't uncomfortable already. We looked at why porn is dangerous. And it is. We also talked about some starting tips to getting out of a porn addiction. If you're struggling with this area, I hope this chapter encouraged you to get help. I hope you'll tell someone and not wait. Porn is just too much of a problem to put off getting out of.

Then we talked about bullying and the least of these in your life. I hope you'll start looking for those in your life that can't help themselves. I hope you'll embrace your responsibility to help those in need, and show Christ's love to them. I hope you won't make excuses, and you won't worry about the consequences. Remember, a man of God charges into battle. Even if it might hurt his reputation.

Finally, we talked about forgiveness. I saved this one for last because it's a tough one. We talked about the difference between forgiveness, justice, and revenge. We looked at the model Jesus gave us for forgiveness. I hope you'll start practicing forgiveness in your life. It's a tough one. And it's going to take some practice. But it's worth it.

You've heard me say it a hundred times by now, but I'm going to say it one more time.

You are a man of God.

Right now. Right now, you're a man of God. I hope you haven't bought into the mentality of "someday" that the whole world is telling you.

Someday, you'll be great at math, but now you're learning

Someday, you'll be great at baseball, but now you're practicing

Someday, you'll be ready to date, but now you're finding yourself

Someday, you'll be ready to drive, but now you have a learners permit

Someday, you'll be ready...

And for some things, that's true. You're probably not ready to get married right now. You're probably not ready to own a million dollar business right now. There are some things that you need to work on first. But being a man of God is not one of them. Accepting your responsibility as Christ's representative on earth is not one of them. Starting to live out your faith is not one of them.

You're ready. I know you are.

There's only one action step for you to take in this chapter. And it's to go out, and change the world. Men of God change the world for the better. And by living out the topics we discussed in this book, you will.

One of my favorite quotes is attributed to Gandhi and it is,

"Be the change you wish to see in the world."

That's my final challenge to you. Go out. Put the things we talked about into practice. And be the change.

NOTES

1) The Editors of Encyclopædia Britannica. "Trench warfare." Encyclopædia Britannica. Encyclopædia Britannica, inc., 2015. Web. 03 Jan. 2017.

2) Guetta, David, and Akon. Sexy bitch. Virgin, 2009. CD.

3) Chan, Francis, and Danae Yankoski. Crazy love: overwhelmed by a relentless God. Colorado Springs, CO: David C. Cook, 2008. Print

4) MacDonald, James. Act like men: 40 days to biblical manhood. Chicago: Moody Publishers, 2014. Print

5) "Chivalry." Wikipedia. Wikimedia Foundation, n.d. Web. 03 Jan. 2017

6) Evans, Tony. Kingdom man: every man's destiny, every woman's dream. Carol Stream, IL: Tyndale House Publishers, 2012. Print

7) "Covenant Eyes." Porn Stats | Covenant Eyes | The Leaders in Accountability Software. N.p., n.d. Web. 03 Jan. 2017

8) "Understanding Addiction." Understanding Addiction: How Addiction Hijacks the Brain. N.p., n.d. Web. 03 Jan. 2017

9) Challies, Tim, and C. H. Spurgeon. Sexual detox: a guide for guys who are sick of porn. Adelphi, MD: Cruciform Press, 2010. Print

10) Struthers, William M. Wired for intimacy: how pornography hijacks the male brain. Downers Grove, IL: IVP, 2009. Print

11) Coogler, R. (Director), & Covington, A. (Writer). (2015). [Motion picture on DVD]. United States of America: Metro-Goldwyn-Mayer

12) Columbus, C. (Director). (2002). Harry Potter and the chamber of secrets [Motion picture]. United States of America: Warner Brothers

13) Gross, Craig, and Steven Luff. Pure eyes: a man's guide to sexual integrity. Grand Rapids, MI: Baker, 2010. Print

14) Stoeker, Fred, and Stephen Arterburn. Every Young Man's Battle: strategies for victory in the real world of sexual temptation. Colorado Springs: WaterBrook Press, 2002. Print

15) The Patriot. Dir. Roland Emmerich. Perf. Mel Gibson. Columbia Pictures., 2000

Cover designed by Cakamura art studio, on 99designs.com

Author photo taken by BlackLevel Photography

THANK YOU...

First and foremost to my wonderful wife. I could not have created this without you. Thank you for your encouragement. Thank you for believing someone would read a book I wrote. Thank you for being so supportive and loving. I love you. Thank you.

To the newest addition of my family. We have not met yet, but I wrote this book for you. I hope it inspires you to be the man God created you to be. Or influences the men in your life. Either way, you have inspired me. Thank you.

To my parents. Who have supported me in so many endeavors both emotionally and financially. Thank you.

To my coach, Kary. Thank you for all that you do. If not for you, this "baby" would not exist. Thank you for allowing me to share my message. Thank you.

To my very good friends at BlackLevel Photography. Thanks for making me look so good. Thank you.

To my editor Elizabeth. Thank you for catching my mistakes, and making me sound more eloquent than I am. Thank you.

To my new friends at Cakamura art studio, who were able to make a vision in my head a reality on the cover of this book. Thank you.

Finally, to you. Whoever you are. Thank you for reading this book. I hope you found it worth your time. Thank you.

ABOUT THE AUTHOR

Andy Buckwalter is a writer and speaker who helps today's teenage men challenge, solidify, and grow their faith so that they can become more of the man God created them to be.

Connect at AndyBuckwalter.com

CPSIA information can be obtained
at www.ICGtesting.com
Printed in the USA
BVOW10s2113140817
492060BV00007B/32/P